Roots *of* Home

Roots *of* Home

OUR JOURNEY TO A NEW OLD HOUSE

RUSSELL VERSACI

Photography by Erik Kvalsvik

The Taunton Press

The Taunton Press
Inspiration for hands-on living®

The Taunton Press, Inc., 63 South Main Street, PO Box 5506,
Newtown, CT 06470-5506
e-mail: tp@taunton.com

Editor: Peter Chapman
Copy editor: Diane Sinitsky
Jacket/Cover design: Stark Design
Interior design: Chika Azuma
Photographer: Erik Kvalsvik, except where noted

Library of Congress Cataloging-in-Publication Data
Versaci, Russell.
  Roots of home : our journey to a new old house / author, Russell
Versaci ; photographer, Erik Kvalsvik.
     p. cm.
  Includes bibliographical references and index.
  ISBN 978-1-56158-867-1 (alk. paper)
  1. Architecture, Domestic--United States. I. Kvalsvik, Erik. II.
Title.
  NA7205.V48 2008
  728'.370973--dc22
                                    2008006715

Printed in Singapore
10 9 8 7 6 5 4 3 2 1

The following name appearing in *Roots of Home* is a trademark:
Lincoln Logs®

For Kathie Friedley, my soul mate and a fine writer,
whose patience and devotion have coached a hack into becoming an author.
She is the heroine in these pages.

ACKNOWLEDGMENTS

Like designing a home, writing a book is a collaboration rather than a solo performance. Many talented hands have made this book possible.

Foremost is photographer Erik Kvalsvik, whose company I have enjoyed in our travels across America. Erik's breathtaking images have brought the story to life and turned the text into a work of art.

Kathie Friedley has been by my side from the beginning, helping to shape my raw ideas, plumbing architects' websites in search of the perfect house, and editing my words as I tried to make sense of what I'd learned. Her stern counsel still echoes in my head: "Don't submit a word without my reviewing it first."

Without editor Peter Chapman, the thread of *Roots of Home* would have unwound long ago. Peter is a gentleman of the old school who shares my love of history. His steady hand and patient critique of every word have refined my rambling tale into readable prose.

I am privileged to have worked with executive editor Steve Culpepper, whose steadfast faith in the concept of *Roots of Home* helped me navigate the corridors of publishing and brought the book to fruition. Along the way, Steve coaxed former publisher Jim Childs into becoming a believer, for whose support I am most grateful. Art director Alison Wilkes and photo editor Wendi Mijal have groomed the text and images into a polished book that is a delight to the eye.

The homes that grace these pages are the work of creative traditional architects whom I am privileged to call colleagues. The unsung heroes of the houses we create are the builders and craftsmen who translate our paper drawings into built homes. Thank you for your talent and commitment to getting the details right.

All of us who practice this trade know that the homes we design would not be possible without clients who share our enthusiasm and devotion to tradition. To all of the families who have opened their homes and allowed me to share their beauty with others, I am most grateful.

Historical advice and words of encouragement have been a vital part of my research into the *Roots of Home*. I am indebted to William Seale, Frank Masson, John Milner, Marc Appleton, Mark Hewitt, John Massengale, Gary Brewer, David Salmela, and Dale Mulfinger, among many others who have contributed to the work.

Final thanks are due to The Historic American Buildings Survey, for the magnificent photographs from their unequaled archives of early American architecture.

CONTENTS

INTRODUCTION

I am an architectural tourist. I like nothing better than traveling somewhere new to look at old houses.

After three decades of touring, I still have an insatiable appetite for the old. I'm drawn by the craftsmanship and wisdom embedded in old houses, by their nobility and grace, even when they are shabby and decayed.

I tour on foot, walking the streets and looking up to study old house character. I record the distinctive features that make them different—what materials they are made of, how the parts go together, where the windows are placed, what shape the roof takes. Slowly these visual impressions add up to a catalog of telling details that define the architecture for me.

I use what I've learned to design "new old houses" —new homes that re-create the authentic character of old houses. I reinterpret the telling details of a classic style using modern building methods. Based on the wisdom of the past, I fashion new old houses that work for modern living.

While working on my first book, *Creating a New Old House,* I was intrigued by the stories behind classic house styles that defined the places I love. I realized that there are reasons why houses look the way they do, that in each place historical factors have shaped house character. Feeling the need to know more about where American houses came from, I began my search into the *Roots of Home.*

My adventure has uncovered layers of history and experience that began in places where European colonists first set foot in America. I call these birthplaces the "Ten Colonial Cradles of Home." In each place, a homegrown blend of customs, climate, and context has matured over generations into a classic style that defines the character of the place.

Respect for the character of place is one of the essential pillars for creating a new old house. A new old house should be attuned to the history, culture, and environment of a place in order to be appropriate there. To create a house that fits in, we must understand where traditions came from, why they look the way they do, and how they have changed over time. Only then can we renew tradition with authenticity.

Today, the best traditional architects are renewing time-tested traditions in new old houses meant for the present. These traditions are constantly evolving. Rather than being dead, historical leftovers, they are living customs, each with a fascinating tale of birth, evolution, and renewal over time. Today, we are simply adding new pages to the story.

This book is a snapshot of America's story of home—where we have come from, what we have learned, and how we are honoring the past in the homes we create today. The story will not end with us, for colorful new chapters will be written as future generations follow in our footsteps. My mission is to record how we got here in the first place, to inspire your quest for a new old house with authentic roots in the past.

I hope that you will enjoy the journey as much as I have.

Footprints of the Past as Blueprints for the Future

"If architecture is the physical evidence of history, certainly history makes a tremendous impact on architecture....Thus if you will understand architecture, you must also know history."
—ALBERT MANUCY, *The Houses of St. Augustine* (1962)

❧

Good houses, whether old or new, start somewhere. They begin with a precedent or a tradition with sturdy roots in the past. Architects like to say they have good bones.

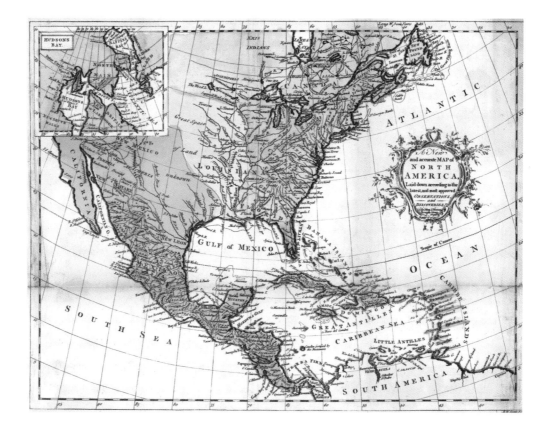

Good bones come from building traditions that have been refined by generations of builders in places with a distinct cultural heritage. Think of visiting an old town such as Nantucket, Charleston, Santa Fe, or New Orleans. What makes these places so special? We marvel at the weathered cottages of Nantucket, the classical piazzas of Charleston, the pink adobe walls of Santa Fe, or the lacy ironwork of New Orleans and realize that classic house styles are what define the character of the places we love.

But where did these styles come from? What makes each one so different? Classic styles were born from a mix of cultural heritage, climate, geography, and natural resources that are unique to a place. I call these historical forces the "roots of home." They have shaped traditions that are the hallmarks of America's favorite places. They are the starting point for building new houses in authentic styles—"new old houses"—that complement the places we love.

In America, we have four centuries of building traditions to explore that provide the rootstock for creating new old houses. From coast to coast, there are regional vernacular styles, such as the New England saltbox, the Pennsylvania stone farmhouse, the Gulf Coast raised cottage, the Texas rock house, and the California *casa*. Each provides a rich source of inspiration for new homes that are timeless classics.

Since colonial times, classic styles have evolved as successive generations have adapted old styles to meet new needs. It is no different today. A new old house should fit into its surroundings, be built to last for generations, and also suit our modern lives by interpreting old traditions in creative new ways. When we create a new old house, we carry the seeds of the past into the present.

To get the details right, we need to understand the origins of American building traditions. To understand the roots of home, we need to begin with history.

BIRTH OF A NATION: LOOKING BACK AT AMERICA

When Christopher Columbus stumbled upon America in 1492, he opened a new world for the great powers of Europe. Since the beginning of the Renaissance, the ambitious monarchs of Spain, France, and England, along with the merchants of Portugal and the Netherlands, had been competing for empire and trade across the globe. In Columbus's wake, the European powers spent the next three centuries jockeying for position, possessions, and ever-larger shares of America.

Spain, France, and England left the greatest legacies. By the dawn of the 17th century, Spain had established a toehold in Florida at St. Augustine (1565); France had planted its flag on the Gulf of St. Lawrence in Acadia (1604); and England had settled a colony in Virginia at Jamestown (1607). With these first tentative forays into colony building, the history of America began.

On the eve of the Revolutionary War, the map of North America shows a continent divided into vast colonial empires. The English controlled the 13 original colonies of the Eastern seaboard; the French, the vast river system of the Mississippi Valley, Great Lakes, and St. Lawrence River; and the Spanish, the Southwest and Alta California. Together the dominions of Spain, France, and England covered four-fifths of the future United States.

OLD-WORLD ROOTS

America's architectural journey began with colonial styles that washed up on our shores in the baggage of European fortune hunters, soldiers, traders, missionaries, reformers, and colonizers. They built homes that blended memory and experience in equal measure, adapting old-world building traditions to the pragmatic requirements of new-world climates, geography, and

Reconstructed at the Frontier Culture Museum of Virginia are historic examples of the old-world roots of American homebuilding, including a 17th-century German fachwerk *farmhouse (right), an Irish fieldstone cottage from 18th-century Ulster (center), and an 18th-century log farmhouse from the Shenandoah Valley of Virginia (left).*

(opposite page) By the time of the American Revolution, the North American continent was divided largely into Spanish, French, and English spheres of influence, with England claiming the Atlantic Coast, France the Mississippi Valley, and Spain the Southwest.

natural resources. Some things worked well, while others had to change. Over time, indigenous regional traditions began to take root that were practical as well as innovative—and distinctly American in flavor.

The styles were also portable. As succeeding generations moved out to the frontier, pioneers brought with them what they had learned. Styles of homebuilding migrated and were transplanted into fresh soil, retaining aspects of their earlier character while being reshaped to fit into new places. Over centuries of slow change, these early colonial roots evolved into classic American styles.

Today we know these styles by their regional identities—New England Colonial, Pennsylvania Dutch, Virginia Tidewater, Carolina Low Country, Louisiana Creole, Southwest Adobe, California Mission, and others. Each style has a rich history for us to explore. By learning their stories and studying their character, we can use what we learn to design new old houses with good bones.

A classic American journey

The pattern of adaptation and survival of old-world traditions is an intriguing part of the story of the American home. Consider the tale of the Pennsylvania Dutch farmhouse, which began in William Penn's Quaker colony in 1682.

Thousands of colonists arrived in Pennsylvania from England, Germany, Scotland, Ireland, and France, lured by the promise of freedom, religious tolerance, and generous land grants. From the woodland wilderness around Philadelphia they carved plots of fertile farmland. On these new farmsteads, settlers built houses like those they had known in the Old Country, tailoring what they knew to fit the rock-strewn soils. They stacked fieldstones into sturdy walls and framed floors and roofs with hewn oak timbers. Their stone farmhouses became known as the "Pennsylvania Dutch" style.

Within a generation, intrepid Pennsylvania pioneers sought greener pastures, migrating south in search of good farmland at bargain prices. By the mid 18th century, thousands of families had traveled down the Great Philadelphia Wagon Road through Maryland and Virginia into the Carolinas and Georgia.

All along the way, they transplanted their religious beliefs, farming practices, decorative arts, and building customs. Historic examples of Pennsylvania stone houses, with their bank barns built into hillsides and pastures outlined in stacked fieldstone walls, can still be seen across the Southern Piedmont.

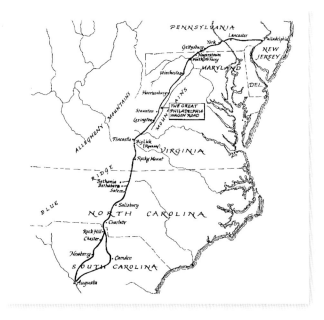

The Great Philadelphia Wagon Road was Pennsylvania's pioneer route that followed the foothills of the Appalachian Mountains through the Valley of Virginia into the Carolinas.

Walnut Grove Plantation (1765) in South Carolina is a classic Southern I-house, a linear two-story house with full front porch that became the favorite farmhouse of 19th-century America.

With each move the newcomers adapted the Pennsylvania farmhouse to accommodate local climates and building materials. They began to use timbers for framing walls, sided them with wooden clapboards, and added porches across the front. Over the years, the Pennsylvania farmhouse absorbed influences from the English colonies of the South, such as a center-hall floor plan and symmetrical facade.

By the beginning of the 19th century, while the roots of the Pennsylvania Dutch style were still visible, the houses had been transformed into something new. From this mix was born the Southern I-house, a simple, symmetrical clapboard house with attached porches. The style was so popular that it migrated well beyond the South, eventually becoming the iconic American farmhouse from coast to coast.

In the American melting pot, there are many similar tales. New Englanders migrated first into New York and then along the Mohawk Trail and Great Lakes into the Old Northwest Territory. The French followed the Ohio and Mississippi Rivers into Kentucky, Missouri, and Arkansas, eventually settling in Louisiana. Spanish missionaries filtered up from Mexico into Texas and the Southwest and along the California coast as far north as San Francisco.

With each of these migrations, colonial traditions were adapted and transformed, adding new chapters to the story of the American home.

When Scots-Irish pioneers such as Hezekiah Alexander migrated south from Pennsylvania to the Carolinas in the mid 18th century, they built homes (left and far left) of fieldstone and timber akin to those they had left behind, transporting earlier roots to new ground.

Ten Colonial Cradles of Home

America's classic home styles were born in 10 regional cradles that lined the edges of North America from Acadia in Canada to California, each region nurturing a distinctive house form. In some cradles one of the European powers played a dominant role, as in Spanish Florida and English Chesapeake Bay. In others, the seeds were sown by several cultures, such as the Gulf Coast, where a blend of French, Spanish, Caribbean, and African traditions took root.

St. Lawrence and Mississippi Valleys

The first French settlement in North America was founded in 1604 in Acadia, now Canada's Maritime Provinces. On the Gulf of St. Lawrence, Samuel de Champlain laid out a fortified village surrounded by wooden palisades to protect the inhabitants. Their houses were made of logs set upright in the ground under steep, bark-covered roofs using a technique called *poteaux-en-terre,* or posts-in-the-ground. This French Colonial house form was built across the frontier as venturesome French explorers, trappers, and missionaries charted the Great Lakes, the Illinois Country, and the Mississippi Valley down to New Orleans.

New England

In 1620, English Pilgrims landed on the shore of Cape Cod and then established Plimoth Plantation on the mainland the following spring. Along the way, they signed the Mayflower Compact, setting down rights and responsibilities to ensure the colony's common good. The Pilgrims built thatched-roof houses of wattle and daub, like the peasant cottages of England, with land set aside for gardens and common pasturage. The homes were arranged in a compact village around a common green, a plan that symbolized the tight-knit

St. Lawrence and Mississippi Valleys: Louis Bolduc House, Ste. Genevieve, Missouri (1785).

New England: John Martin House, Swansea, Massachusetts (1728).

rules of the Pilgrim community and set a pattern for New England towns for the next 200 years.

Hudson Valley

Sixteen years after Henry Hudson's 1609 voyage up the river that bears his name, the Dutch settled the colony of New Netherland. In the towns of New York and Albany, Dutchmen built brick townhouses like the ones they remembered from the streets of Amsterdam, Leiden, and Utrecht. As Dutch settlers moved up the Hudson and out to Long Island and New Jersey, they built farmhouses of stone and wood shingles, resembling those of the Dutch and Flemish lowlands. Soon the tall, steep roofs of the Low Countries were replaced with a new form learned from the English—the gambrel roof with a flared eave—and the iconic Dutch Colonial style was born.

Delaware Valley

The colony of New Sweden was founded on the Delaware River in 1638, lasting just 17 years before being absorbed into Pennsylvania. Even though short-lived, the Swedish colony left a lasting architectural legacy—the log cabin. The Swedish log cabin, built of logs stacked horizontally, became the first home for settlers across the American frontier. In 1682 New Sweden became part of William Penn's haven for English Quakers. Soon Rhineland Germans were attracted to the Quaker colony's religious tolerance and pacifism. While Quakers built brick townhouses in Philadelphia like those of Georgian London, German farmers cleared the wilderness and harvested fieldstones to build houses in a style that became known as Pennsylvania Dutch.

Chesapeake Bay

England's first claim in the New World was Virginia. Begun in 1607 at Jamestown, the colony reached

Hudson Valley: Pieter Claessen Wyckoff House, Brooklyn, New York (1652).

Delaware Valley: Peaceable Farm, New Hope, Pennsylvania (1930–35).

TEN COLONIAL

America's classic home styles were born in ten regional cradles that

Alta California

Alta California was the last Spanish frontier, where a chain of 21 missions was created from 1769 through 1823 along the coastline from San Diego to Sonoma.

Southwest Borderlands

Starting in the early 17th century, the Spanish crisscrossed the Southwest borderlands founding presidios, missions, and pueblos from Arizona to Texas.

Gulf Coast

Settled by the French at New Orleans in 1718, the Gulf Coast attracted French and Spanish Creoles, Acadians from Canada, and free blacks from the Caribbean.

Florida Peninsula

The Spanish established North America's first settlement in Florida at St. Augustine in 1565, as well as a chain of missions linked through Tallahassee to Pensacola.

Carolina Low Country

The Carolina Low Country and its tidewater coast were first settled in Charleston in 1670 by English planters with roots in the Caribbean islands.

CRADLES OF HOME

nurtured distinctive house forms rooted in Old World traditions.

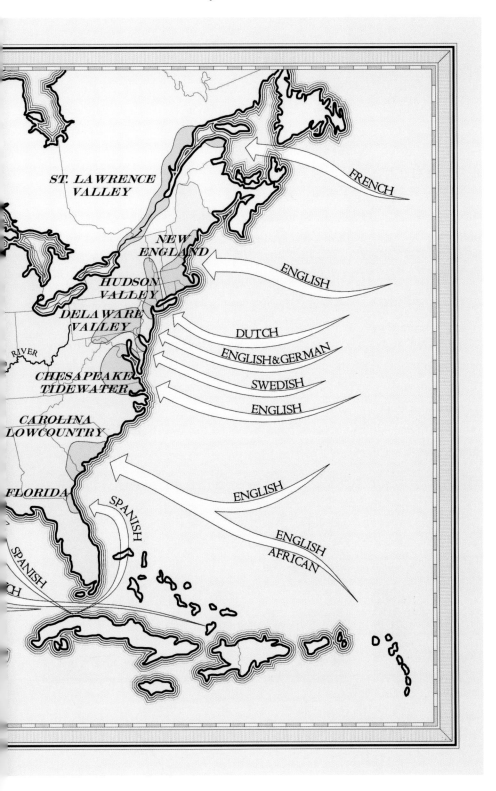

St Lawrence and Mississippi Valleys

The first French settlement was founded at Port-Royal on the Gulf of St. Lawrence in 1604, followed by exploration of the Great Lakes and Mississippi Valley.

New England

English Pilgrims established Plimoth Plantation on the New England coast in 1621 and spurred the founding of compact villages from Connecticut to Maine.

Hudson Valley

The Dutch founded New Amsterdam in 1624, while French Huguenots and Flemish Walloons settled into the Hudson Valley from New Jersey to upstate New York.

Delaware Valley

The Delaware Valley was first home to New Sweden (1638) and later Pennsylvania (1682), a haven for English Quakers as well as German and Scots-Irish émigrés.

Chesapeake Bay

On Chesapeake Bay, the Virginia colony was founded by the English at Jamestown in 1607, followed by Maryland established at St. Mary's City in 1634.

from Savannah to the Hudson River. Its settlers were English squires, merchants, artisans, and their indentured servants who built Virginia plantations of clapboard and brick in the image of English manors. In 1634 Lord Baltimore received a tract of land carved from Virginia above the Potomac River and founded Maryland. He sold large parcels of this land to his fellow Cavaliers, who, like their countrymen in Virginia, built houses around Chesapeake Bay in a style best known today from Colonial Williamsburg.

Carolina Low Country

In the 1670s, English planters left Barbados to resettle in the Carolina colony and brought Anglo-Caribbean townhouses and plantations to the tidewater Low Country. Charleston, the first settlement, became a center of trade between London, the Caribbean, and New England, and wealthy Charleston merchants built elegant townhouses in the latest English styles. The Charleston single house with its two-story classical piazza merged English classical and Caribbean traditions in a new form. In the surrounding Low Country, landowners became wealthy growing rice, cotton, and indigo and built plantation houses with raised foundations and open verandas like those they had known in the Caribbean.

Florida Peninsula

Founded in 1565, St. Augustine was the earliest cradle of colonial architecture and the seat of America's first permanent colony. Spaniard Don Pedro Menendez de Aviles, a naval commander, built the town around a plaza and mission church as dictated by the Spanish colonial Laws of the Indies. The early houses were cypress planks covered with palm thatch roofs. Later, sturdier homes were made of *coquina,* or shell stone, and of tabby, a primitive form of concrete. When the English took control of St. Augustine in 1763, they imported traditions from the West Indies, creating

Chesapeake Bay: West St. Mary's Manor, St. Mary's, Maryland (1700–30).

Carolina Low Country: Magnolia Mound, Baton Rouge, Louisiana (1786).

Anglo-Caribbean houses with verandas and pitched roofs that came to symbolize the city.

Gulf Coast

For most of the 17th century, French explorers, fur traders, and missionaries worked their way inland from the St. Lawrence and Great Lakes, establishing forts and trading posts. The explorer René-Robert Cavelier de La Salle traveled down the Mississippi to the Gulf of Mexico, claimed the Mississippi basin for France, and named the new territory *La Louisiane.* Founded in 1718, New Orleans became a thriving center for trade, attracting French and Spanish Creoles, Acadians from French Canada, Haitian slaves, and freed blacks. Each group contributed their traditions to the Gulf Coast's rich brew of French plantations, Spanish townhouses, Creole cottages, and Afro-Caribbean shotgun houses.

Southwest Borderlands

Beginning in 1610, the Spanish created chains of pre-sidios, missions, and pueblos to protect New Spain's northern borderlands and convert the Native Americans to Catholicism. The city of Santa Fe became a mission center where Franciscan friars taught the Pueblo Indians to build houses of sun-baked adobe bricks, using a traditional method learned in Mexico that proved well suited to the parched desert climate. In Texas, the Spanish established another mission chain, with San Antonio as its center, to thwart the French in Louisiana. There the Spanish built splendid churches with carved decoration fashioned from soft Texas limestone.

Alta California

Although the Spanish had explored the California coastline for 200 years, they did not begin a chain of frontier missions like those in New Mexico and Texas until 1769. Founded by Father Junipero Serra, the mission at Monterey became the capital of Spanish California. After Mexican independence in 1821, the church's authority began to wane, and powerful California ranchers took over the mission lands. They built simple adobe farmhouses with baked tile roofs, which, though spare looking on the outside, were cool and comfortable on the inside, with continuous covered walkways that surrounded a courtyard garden. Adapted to the dry, hot climate, this style endured to become the classic California ranch house.

(top) Florida Peninsula: Ximenez-Fatio House, St. Augustine, Florida (1798).

(bottom) Gulf Coast: James Pitot House, New Orleans, Louisiana (1799).

ROOTS OF HOME

The story of the American home begins with these journeys across time, but it doesn't end there. The adventure has taken new twists and turns over four centuries as classic styles have evolved over time.

The story continued at the turn of the 20th century when grand spectacles such as the Philadelphia Centennial (1876) and the Panama-California Exposition (1915) sparked new interest in old building traditions. Architects of the time revived early colonial houses with creative imagination in Colonial Revival styles. Another chapter is being written today, as architects create new old houses to suit life in the modern age. For inspiration, they are returning to living traditions that continue to grow over time.

This book is a journey of discoveries. In its pages we will trace the roots of home—the origins of American house styles that are enduring classics. We will travel with the first settlers as they adapted building skills honed in the Old Country to their new land. We will trace changes made over centuries as succeeding generations modified freshly minted customs. Finally, we will visit the latest chapter in the evolution of classic styles, looking at new old houses designed by today's best traditional architects.

Along the way, we will discover what gives a house good bones. We will uncover footprints of the past that provide blueprints for new old houses that are pleasing to the eye and satisfying to the soul—classic American houses that look and feel like home.

Southwest Borderlands: Fulton Ranch, Wise County, Texas (2001).

Alta California: Rancho Olivas, Ventura, California (1852).

THE DANIEL BOONE HOMESTEAD

The homestead of Daniel Boone's birth is a 1731 fieldstone farmhouse built in the Pennsylvania Dutch country west of Philadelphia. Altered over several generations, today the restored farmhouse shows the straightforward layers of additions that make these stone houses distinctive classics.

The Boone Homestead began as a log cabin that grew through three additions, blending walls of fieldstone with German pent roofs and American porches. Built of local reddish brown sandstone, the walls are irregular rubblework with larger squared corner blocks. The double-hung sash windows are framed into the stonework with wide casing boards and paneled shutters. It was customary for the Pennsylvania Dutch to limewash their stone walls to protect them from the weather or, as in the Boone Homestead, to coat only the wall under the porch roof white to brighten and keep it clean.

Like many intrepid Pennsylvania pioneers, Daniel Boone's family left the Oley Valley in the 1750s when their land began to decline in productivity. They migrated to the South down the Great Philadelphia Wagon Road, following the Appalachian Mountains through the Shenandoah Valley into the Carolinas. For a few shillings, the Boones traded several hundred acres in Pennsylvania for a square mile of land in the Yadkin Valley of North Carolina, transplanting their Pennsylvania Dutch roots into new soil.

(top left) The fieldstone porch walls of many Pennsylvania Dutch farmhouses were painted with white limewash to brighten them and keep them clean.

(top right) The interior walls of the farmhouse were plastered with a smooth, durable lime finish, while the floors and ceilings were made of heavy hewn oak timbers and floorboards.

(left) Built of reddish brown Schuylkill Valley sandstone, the Daniel Boone Homestead (1731) typifies the fieldstone farmhouses of the Pennsylvania Dutch country, with trademark pent eaves that protect the wall below.

1

OUR SPANISH HERITAGE

SOULS FOR GOD, GOLD FOR COUNTRY

"We Americans have yet to really learn our own antecedents . . .
We tacitly abandon ourselves to the notion that our United States have been
fashioned from the British Islands only . . . which is a very great mistake."

—WALT WHITMAN, *The Spanish Element in Our Nationality* (1883)

As America came of age in the late 19th century, Walt Whitman lamented our country's ignorance of its true origins, for it was the Spanish who really founded America, not the English. A century before the English first made landfall at Jamestown in 1607, the Spanish had already thoroughly explored and exploited the riches of the New World.

Spain was the undisputed superpower of 16th-century Europe, boasting unimaginable riches looted from its New World conquests to lord over its rivals—Portugal, England, France, and the Netherlands. With the largest merchant fleet, the most fearsome soldiers, a centralized government, and a steady rein on the Catholic Church, Spain seemed invincible.

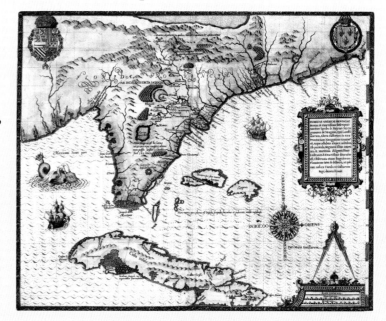

THE NEW-WORLD PRIZE

Confident in its strength, Spain eagerly followed Columbus's voyage of 1492 to plunder the treasures of the Americas. Columbus had brought back news of limitless gold and countless slaves for the taking. By 1600, the Spanish had sacked the ancient civilizations of the Inca and Maya and established thriving colonial outposts in the West Indies and Central America. In New Spain, Mexico City was the provincial capital of a self-governing Spanish state and home to the powerful Council of the Indies.

During the 17th century, most of North America was explored by Spanish adventurers who crisscrossed the continent in search of gold. In the 30 years after Ponce de Leon set foot in *La Florida* in 1513, Cabeza de Vaca wandered from Florida to Baja California, Francisco Vasquez de Coronado trekked the Southwest, and Hernando de Soto explored the Southeast from Virginia to the Mississippi. They were unimpressed with what they found. De Soto called it "the worst country that is warmed by the sun." He saw only shallow harbors, barren soils, and recalcitrant natives. But most damning of all, he found no gold.

PRESIDIOS, MISSIONS, AND PUEBLOS

Discouraged, the Spanish turned away from establishing permanent settlements toward defending their North American claims and converting the natives to Christianity. Spain's colonial outposts were principally fortified chains of presidios, missions, and pueblos rather than pilgrim colonies. They relied on Dominican, Franciscan, and Jesuit missionaries to spread Spanish dominion, often settling in areas with established Indian populations.

Their system of colonization began with military conquest, followed by the establishment of missions to educate and convert the Indians, then a civil administration to provide ongoing governance. But the Spaniards never really came to stay. Most of their outposts were sparsely manned by small bands of soldiers and padres who enlisted for a few short years and then moved on. The few colonists who followed them were mostly men without Spanish wives who took Indian women as concubines.

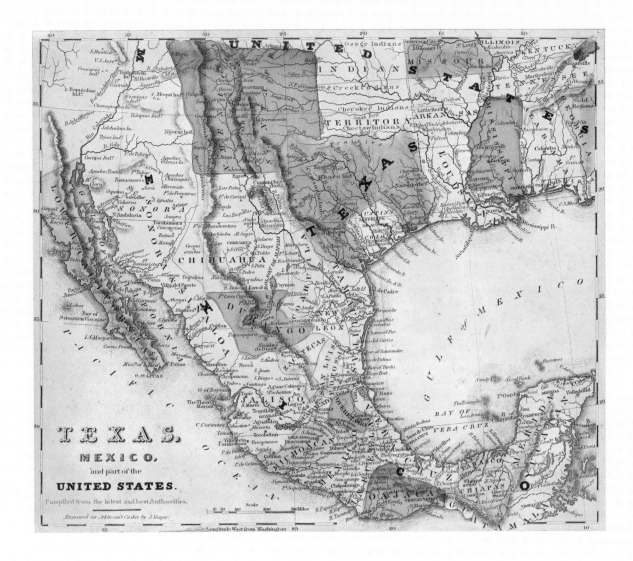

Adobe Casas, Mighty Churches

Spaniards came to North America by way of the Spanish West Indies, where they had learned to adapt their old-world building skills to the new continent. The oldest city in America, the port town of St. Augustine, Florida, was founded in 1565 as a garrison to protect Spain's treasure fleet as it sailed the trade winds through the Straits of Florida toward Seville.

The early settlers of Florida imported the construction techniques they had developed in Hispaniola (Santo Domingo) and Cuba. Their first houses were built of native cedar or cypress frames set in the ground,

covered by plank walls and thatched roofs of palmetto leaves. Later, the Spanish built walls using a primitive form of concrete known as tabby, which was made by pouring an oyster shell mortar into wooden forms. Later still, they quarried blocks of coral rock cut from the coastal barrier islands, called *coquina*, and built more substantial stone houses, as well as forts such as Castillo San Marco in St. Augustine.

The Spanish capital of New Mexico was founded at Santa Fe in 1610 to govern the territory of the Pueblo Indians. In New Mexico, the Spanish refined the mud-building techniques of the natives by stacking blocks of sun-dried adobe bricks into thick walls, beneath a *(opposite page) In the early 18th century, Spanish missionaries crossed Texas to found missions as a bulwark against French incursions from the Mississippi Valley. The chain of missions along the Camino Real from Mexico City to East Texas was headquartered in San Antonio.*

(below) Casa de Estudillo, built in San Diego in 1827, displays the telling details of the early Spanish casas of California. Its walls are made of sun-baked adobe bricks covered by a roof of red clay tiles.

mud-covered roof of crossed timbers and sticks. As in the provincial houses built in New Spain, the Spaniards used stone and clay where they could find them. They introduced the Indians to woodworking tools for building doors, windows, and carved decorative details.

In the 1690s, as French settlements in the Mississippi Valley threatened New Spain's borderlands, the Spaniards reinforced their claims by founding a chain of missions across East Texas. San Antonio began life in 1718 as the major presidio and mission along the Camino Real, or Royal Road, that traversed East Texas. Guided by Franciscan friars, Indian converts built mighty churches as fortresslike centerpieces for mission grounds such as the Alamo. These were simplified versions of the Baroque cathedrals of New Spain, made of thick adobe walls or quarried limestone blocks decorated with crude facsimiles of Spanish ornament.

FINAL FRONTIER

By the late 18th century, Spanish missionaries reached the coastline of Alta California, where the padres transplanted new-world lessons learned over 200 years to the Pacific frontier. The missions and presidios of California showcase these mature Spanish building traditions. Adobe brick construction, cut stone masonry, and fired clay tile roofs were old hat by then, to which the friars added carved woodwork and chiseled stone decoration.

The rediscovery of our Spanish heritage also began in California. A century after the missions were founded, enterprising boosters reinvented the state in the Spanish mold with houses, schools, and public buildings inspired by California's colonial past. Thereafter, Spanish colonial architecture took its rightful place as an equal in America's story of home.

St. Augustine Style

*"The houses [of St. Augustine] are built quite after the Spanish fashion,
with flat roofs and few windows . . . Almost every house
has its little garden, of which splendid lemon and orange
trees are not the least ornaments."*
—William Bartram, *Travels* (1791)

The spirit of Old Florida lives on in St. Augustine, where the Spanish first settled in North America a half century before the English set foot in Jamestown. The houses of St. Augustine are a layered legacy of more than four centuries of living by Spanish, English, and American owners. On the Florida Panhandle, a new St. Augustine-style house designed by architect Jason Dunham of Cooper Johnson Smith draws on Spanish and Anglo-Caribbean traditions from Florida's colonial era.

unham's design is built in the new town of Rosemary Beach. The town is a landmark in the renaissance of traditional neighborhoods called New Urbanism, where communities are walkable and have an old-fashioned sense of place. Arranged in a spider's web of avenues, alleys, and boardwalks built around a town square, Rosemary Beach is a village of traditional homes and shops that reinvents the diverse urban character of Old St. Augustine.

Rosemary Beach is a new traditional neighborhood on the Florida Panhandle planned as a walkable community of compact house lots facing narrow streets and boardwalks. Its character is reminiscent of historic St. Augustine.

COQUINA STONE AND STREET BALCONIES

Settled by the Spanish and christened San Agustin de la Florida in 1565, St. Augustine's natural harbor offered protection for the treasure fleet that sailed the Spanish Main. The city was founded by Pedro Menendez de Aviles, a Spanish naval commander who was given a kingdom in return for his loyal service to the crown. To La Florida he brought a mix of sailors, soldiers, and settlers from Cuba, Mexico, and Spain. He laid out the town according to King Phillip II's Laws of the Indies of 1573, the Spanish system for a grid of streets and building lots formally arranged around a plaza and parish church.

The first Spanish homes were made of cypress, cedar, and palm—woods that were readily available in St. Augustine. From the Timucua Indians the Spaniards learned to build simple, round palm huts with walls covered in cane mats. Next, they tried cypress posts set into the ground, sided with vertical planks called *tablas* and thatched with palm leaves. But wooden houses were no match for the intense humidity and termite-infested soils of Florida. Those that didn't rot were destroyed by Sir Francis Drake, who burned St. Augustine to the ground in 1586. Leveled again in 1702 by Sir Thomas Moore's English marauders, the Spaniards finally turned to what they knew best: stone.

For centuries in Spain's rock-strewn provinces, stone had been the material of choice for building a farmhouse, or *casa de campo*. Fieldstones gathered from the ground or nearby ledges were stacked into walls mortared together with mud and coated inside and out with brilliant white limewash. More sophisticated

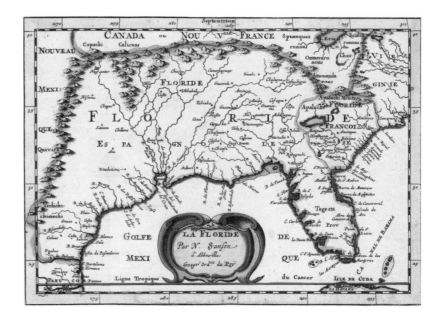

Seventeenth-century Spanish Florida bordered the Gulf of Mexico from the Florida Peninsula to the Rio Grande.

urban townhouses were built of chiseled stone blocks. Thatch or stone slabs covered the shallow-pitched roofs of provincial farmhouses, while finer homes had roofs of baked clay barrel tiles.

In St. Augustine, the Spanish found ledges of coral shellstone, called coquina, on nearby Anastasia Island. They shaped coquina stone into simple, sturdy block walls that were one story tall, then covered them with flat roofs of clay supported by wooden beams called *vigas*. The Spanish also developed a primitive form of concrete called *tapia*, or tabby, a mixture of crushed shells, sand, lime, and water poured into wooden molds to cast solid walls. Whether made of stone or tabby, the plain walls were plastered with clay-lime mortar and painted with limewash for weatherproofing.

The Spaniards built masonry houses for 200 years in St. Augustine until the English took over in 1763. From then on, the town became one of layered history.

The street balconies on 18th-century British West Indies houses were the inspiration for Jason Dunham's porch balcony design, with shutter blinds hung between posts to shield the porch from sun, wind, and rain.

The West Indies tradition of adding a second-floor street balcony to old Spanish casas was adopted by the English after 1763. St. Augustine's balconies are cantilevered out from the wall on floor beams, suspending a private sitting porch above the narrow street below.

Rather than tearing down the old Spanish casas, the English improvised on top of them with their own traditions. They added second stories of wood and covered the new walls with clapboard siding, a building technique they had used on plantation houses in the British West Indies.

The English grafted another centuries-old West Indies tradition onto the old Spanish houses—the suspended balcony. St. Augustine's balconies are cantilevered over the street on second-floor beams that run through the walls, creating private sitting porches that have no support posts to block the narrow streets below. Today these street balconies are the hallmark of the St. Augustine style.

✦ WORDSMITH ✦

• tablas •

A *tablas* house was built of poles set directly into the ground or of heavy hewn logs braced into a timber frame, covered with riven (hand-split) or pit-sawn planks (*tablas*). The plank walls were laid horizontally or vertically and fastened to the frame with wrought-iron nails. Sometimes a coating of tar pitch was applied to protect the wood against the weather.

A FUSION OF ST. AUGUSTINE STYLES

Architect Dunham's house in Rosemary Beach tips its hat to St. Augustine's layering of building traditions in a loose interpretation of old Spanish casas and West Indies plantation houses. The new house is tall and lanky, stretching sturdy Spanish masonry walls into slender stucco piers that march around the outside. This colonnade of white storklike legs reaches 15 ft. high to support a second story of airy West Indies-style wooden porches.

Behind the stucco piers, the core of the house is a long rectangle of white stucco walls that enclose the first-floor rooms. The walls are tall to match the height of the colonnade, and the windows are also oversized. Each double-hung window is much larger than the small openings of old Spanish casas. These were simple cutouts filled in with a grille of wooden spindles, called

A row of tall white stucco piers lifts the house in the air on sturdy, slender legs to support a second story of wooden porches enclosed by airy West Indies-style plantation shutters.

(opposite page) The centerpiece of the Rosemary Beach house is a tall fireplace and wraparound staircase that separates the living and dining rooms from the guest bedroom.

a *reja*, rather than with window glass. On the inside, the openings were closed tight by wooden shutters to provide privacy, security, and a layer of winter warmth.

The second floor of the new house, styled like a West Indies plantation, seems light and delicate compared with the masonry walls below. Its deep porches are made of square wooden posts filled in with plantation shutters, or blinds, painted dark spruce green. A traditional shading device still used throughout the Caribbean, the shutters swing open to bring daylight and sea breezes into second-floor bedrooms.

A steep umbrella roof hipped at both ends spreads over the porches to protect them from the sudden downpours and hot sun of subtropical Florida. Many early Spanish casas had flat roofs of clay or of tabby tiles, called *azoteas*, which were installed over wooden vigas and sloped just enough to drain off rainwater. English planters imported the umbrella roof covered in split cypress shingles from the Caribbean. Today most roofs

in coastal Florida, like the roof on Dunham's house, are sheet metal coated with zinc that weathers to a soft sheen.

Translating traditions

The main entrance to the house is a cathedral-like archway formed by two white columns topped with curved wooden brackets. The architect designed this bold archway to interrupt the horizontal line of the facade with a vertical frame around the front door. Steps lead from the street to the doorway, passing through a low terrace wall with simple bench seats cast in place along the sidewalk.

The stair steps and terrace floor are made of terra-cotta-colored concrete finished to look like large tile pavers. An Old St. Augustine tradition, paving for outdoor pathways and interior floors was often made of scored tabby concrete. Tabby mortar was poured over a thick base of shells or stone chips, troweled smooth, and then sealed with several coats of linseed oil.

(far left) Simple bench seats cast in place along the sidewalk sit below the colonnade of white stucco piers. The half-moon cut-outs under the seats are a clever architectural device used to drain rainwater into the sand beneath the house.

(left) Deep porches that open out from the bedrooms are carved into the second floor behind square wooden posts.

(opposite page) An archway of wooden brackets sitting atop two white stucco piers creates a tall frame for the front entrance to the house.

A string of half-moon cutouts punched through the terrace wall creates a decorative detail with a serious purpose. Because the landscape code at Rosemary Beach requires that rainwater be drained under the house rather than into the street, the architect came up with an ingenious solution: Cut scuppers through the foundation to drain water into the thirsty beach sand beneath the house.

Room for gardens is limited on the small lots in the community because the landscape code reserves areas for native plantings. Dunham managed these limits by creating a chain of linked garden rooms around the house—a tiny version of the private interior courtyards of Old St. Augustine. Most delightful is a narrow patio

garden with a lily pool running down the middle, beneath a wooden arbor that makes the space feel private even though it is right next to the street.

Casual seaside vernacular

Inside the new old house, few traces of colonial times remain other than faint echoes of the classic St. Augustine floor plan. The traditional layout was a long rectangle of rooms with a covered porch cut into the backside called a *loggia*. The loggia sheltered the main doorway and created an outdoor living room that was protected and comfortable most of the year. In the Rosemary Beach house, the space that would have been the loggia is filled in by the kitchen and surrounded by a wall of windows.

The living room and dining room are joined together through a wide cased doorway that makes the public rooms more casual and informal.

*A narrow patio garden filled with a lily pool and wooden arbor boasts an outdoor fireplace knit into the garden walls at its far end.
Grapevines straddle the arbor to provide shade and flowering greenery, just as they did inside the courtyards of Old St. Augustine.*

The interiors are furnished in a contemporary sea-side vernacular that is light and bright. The first floor is loosely split into public and private rooms divided down the middle by a staircase and fireplace. From the front door, one looks straight through the living room toward the kitchen windows. Wide-framed openings connect the living room, dining room, and kitchen so that they work together as one room. Sunlight pours in through large windows, flooding the interior of this casual house by the sea.

ICONS OF OLD ST. AUGUSTINE

In St. Augustine's historic district, restored houses record the legacy of Spanish, English, and American layers. While no wooden houses from the earliest period survive, many of the Spanish casas made of coquina stone are still with us, often underneath additions that obscure the way they first looked. Today this history inspires new old houses like the one Dunham designed for Rosemary Beach.

Among dozens of well-preserved houses, the Fernandez-Llambias House is the most memorable portrait of a true Spanish Colonial home. Built after the English siege, during the second Spanish period of 1702 to 1763, the earliest part of the house is a single-story casa made of coquina stone plastered with lime-and-sand mortar.

After the English occupation began in 1763, a second story was added onto the house beneath a hipped roof

The original Fernandez-Llambias House was altered after 1763 with the addition of an Anglo-Caribbean street balcony. Perhaps the most photographed historic detail in the city, this street balcony is the icon of St. Augustine style.

(left) Located where the loggia *would have been in a traditional St. Augustine house, the kitchen is bathed in sunlight coming through the windows that surround the room on three sides.*

covered in wood shingles. One of St. Augustine's classic cantilevered wooden balconies hangs off the old walls. The hewn beams that support the porch project out over the street to hold up square posts and a hipped roof.

The Gonzalez-Alvarez House is a clear precedent for Dunham's new old house. Known in St. Augustine as the Oldest House, its Spanish walls were built of coquina stone, with a timberframe second story added by the English. Typical of late 18th-century English construction, the upper walls are covered with beveled clapboards painted gray-green, making the Oldest House the perfect example of the city's fusion of Spanish and Anglo-Caribbean influences.

Spanish courtyards

In Old St. Augustine, the courtyard was the center of daily life—the *placita*—both a workroom and a gathering place when the weather was fair. Building lots were deep enough so that stables, storehouses, a cook house,

a bread oven, a well, and a privy could fill out the back of the plot. This left an open patio between the house and its outbuildings, filled with a kitchen garden and fruit trees and often centered on a water fountain.

The De Mesa-Sanchez House, built around 1764, has one of the finest St. Augustine courtyards. Stone walls and a string of outbuildings enclose the patio, now paved in bricks. Simple plastered arches line the first-floor loggia to create a covered outdoor terrace and entrance porch. Above the loggia, there is a wooden balcony off the second-floor parlor.

Looking at this courtyard, one can see where Dunham found the inspiration for the pillars and porches at Rosemary Beach. He has translated the loggia into a row of tall columns and reinvented the second-floor balcony as a wraparound porch with plantation shutters. The classic St. Augustine patio also inspired the design of the small courtyards, gardens, and water features that surround the Dunham house.

The walls of the Gonzalez-Alvarez House trace layers of building history, from early Spanish walls of stucco-covered coquina *stone to late 18th-century English timberframe additions of painted wood clapboards.*

A typical St. Augustine house had no front door on the street. The real front door was located off the courtyard under a covered loggia *like this one on the De Mesa-Sanchez House (1764).*

St. Augustine Style Comes of Age

The 1920s Spanish Colonial Revival ignored the real Spanish roots of Florida, opting instead for a picturesque stage-set version of the Old World. Architect Addison Mizner (1872–1933) costumed Palm Beach in the image of the Riviera, while impresario George Merrick (1886–1942) painted his suburb of Coral Gables in "Spanish, Venetian, Moorish, Italian, and other similarly harmonious types of architecture." The idea of looking at the Spanish plazas, churches, and casas of Old St. Augustine didn't even occur to them.

Scant attention was paid to the beauty of St. Augustine's old houses until historian and restorer Albert Manucy wrote his eye-opening study, *The Houses of St. Augustine 1565–1821,* in 1962. A native of the city with Spanish family roots, Manucy pieced together the evolution of house styles from the Spanish to the American periods. His meticulous research into the design details, construction techniques, and materials used to build the early houses from foundations to roofs served as a catalyst for architectural preservation in St. Augustine.

Not until the 1990s did architects awaken to the design potential of the St. Augustine style. At that time Andres Duany and Elizabeth Plater-Zyberk created the New Urbanist community of Windsor in Vero Beach, Florida, and coded the characteristics of the style into design guidelines for new houses. Their own 1995 design for Windsor House draws straight from the plain stucco walls, hipped roofs, street balconies, and enclosed courtyards of the old town. Since then, other talented traditional architects have followed their lead in homes designed for Seaside, Rosemary Beach, and their imitators on the "Design Coast" of the Florida Panhandle.

The tall stucco piers and shuttered balconies of the Rosemary Beach house translate the layered character of St. Augustine's historic stucco-and-wood houses into an updated interpretation of the classic style.

The gardens surrounding the new old house are a miniature version of the interior courtyards of Old St. Augustine. Entered through a gate cut into the enclosing walls, several small courtyard gardens are linked together in a chain of outdoor rooms.

(right) Andres Duany and Elizabeth Plater-Zyberk's 1995 design for Windsor House renewed architectural interest in the plain stucco walls, hipped roofs, street balconies, and enclosed courtyards that are classic features of Old St. Augustine.

(below) French doors open onto the second-floor balcony outside the master bedroom of the Rosemary Beach house.

XIMENEZ-FATIO HOUSE

The St. Augustine house of Andres Ximenez was built in 1798 on a lot first developed soon after the city's founding. A home site for many generations, it has seen a succession of structures from wattle-and-daub to oyster-shell tabby. Typical of the fusion of Spanish and English styles in the 18th century, the present house is made of coquina shellstone sawed into blocks and stuccoed, with an umbrella roof of cypress shingles and a balcony cantilevered over the street.

Ximenez was a shopkeeper who built his house as a market and tavern with storehouses and a separate kitchen in the backyard, complete with one of the few surviving brick baking ovens. As on many St. Augustine houses, the entrance door is through a loggia facing the inner courtyard. With its stone walls plastered in brilliant white stucco, typical of St. Augustine's finest homes, the Ximenez-Fatio House served as a model for the stucco walls of the new Rosemary Beach house.

(far left) Made of coquina *stone blocks covered in stucco, the Ximenez-Fatio House represents the mature St. Augustine style with Spanish, English, and American layers. Its street balcony reflects Anglo-Caribbean influences, while the roof dormers are American additions.*

(left) Dining room of the Ximenez-Fatio House.

(opposite page) The bright, airy first-floor parlor has windows on two long sides of the narrow room to draw sunlight and cooling breezes through the house.

SPANISH MISSION REVIVAL

"When Texas is populated and governed by good laws, it will be one of the most enviable places in the world, in which it doubtless will play a brilliant role."
—JOSÉ ENRIQUE DE LA PEÑA, *La Rebelión de Texas* (1836)

As every schoolchild knows, "Remember the Alamo" is the rallying cry of Texas. Fought in San Antonio in 1836, the battle of the Alamo pitted rebels facing overwhelming odds against the Republic of Mexico in a legendary battle of courage and grit. From that time on, the Spanish mission of San Antonio de Valero has been a shrine to Texas liberty. Nicknamed the "Alamo" for its splendid grove of cottonwoods, the mission church is one of five that the Spanish built in 18th-century San Antonio—the mission cradle of Texas.

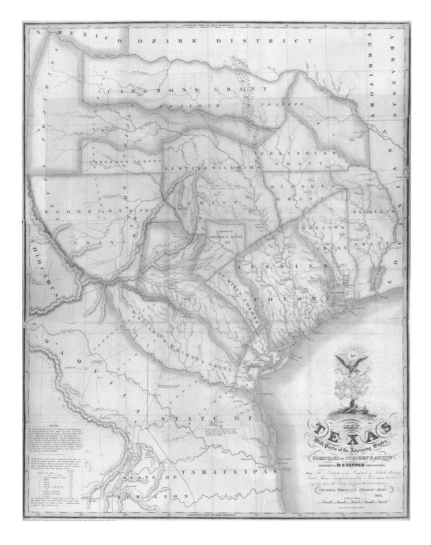

IN THE LAND OF LOS TEJAS

The Alamo, founded in 1718, was the first mission established in the San Antonio River Valley, one of a chain of Spanish missions north of the Rio Grande. San Antonio was the capital of the territory that became Texas, named for the native Indians the Spaniards called *los Tejas*, meaning "friends."

The abundant water and timber of the San Antonio area had long attracted Spanish explorers. The valley became a resting place for Franciscan friars as they trekked east across Texas to build missions as a line of defense against French forays from Louisiana. But the East Texas missions withered under French and Indian

In the mesquite and sagebrush savannah south of San Antonio, architect Michael Imber has created a new hunting ranch called Rancho dos Vidas inspired by the bell towers and red clay tile roofs of the Texas missions. The dusty rose stucco walls of Rancho dos Vidas enclose a hacienda buttressed against a hillside like a fortified Spanish presidio. Built in a wild landscape setting as a self-sufficient oasis, the new house is a spiritual descendant of the Spanish Colonial missions.

The mission of San Antonio de Valero, better known as the Alamo, was founded in 1718, one of five missions that the Spanish built in 18th-century San Antonio. Its decorative portico of classical columns was probably carved by a sculptor recruited for the commission from Mexico.

attacks, frequent droughts, and malaria, and by 1731 three of them had been relocated to San Antonio. There the missions flourished for 60 years, blessed by fruitful farmland and peaceful coexistence between Spanish settlers and Coahuiltecan Indians.

Spanish Colonial architecture had evolved in New Spain for two centuries before it was transplanted to Texas. In the borderlands, the Spaniards favored pragmatic construction over architectural display, largely because they were building in a primitive wilderness. There were few ornamental details beyond an expressive front door and an occasional mission belfry, or *campanario*, except for those crafted by stone carvers recruited from Mexico.

In the sun-parched Southwest, the Spanish perfected building stout walls of mud-covered adobe or stone for protection and insulation. They used arcades of half-round arches for covered porches and passageways. Windows were small, simple openings cut through the walls, designed to minimize heat intrusion and keep the interiors cool. Roofs were covered in mission tiles made of fired red clay shaped into half-round barrels.

A New Hacienda on the Range

At Rancho dos Vidas, Michael Imber has translated the architecture of San Antonio's missions into a new hacienda designed like the grand country estates of New Spain. A hacienda was a manor house surrounded by thousands of acres and hundreds of inhabitants, set up as an independent community with its own church, school, store, and post office.

Imber's new hacienda stands proud and alone in the South Texas backcountry. Its stucco walls, stained the color of poached salmon, shelter the house in the hardscrabble landscape. The thick masonry walls absorb the Texas heat, promising cool sanctuary inside, while windows and doors are deeply recessed to provide shade from the sun.

Mission architecture in Texas was pragmatic rather than decorative because the friars were building in a primitive wilderness. There were few ornamental details beyond a sculptural espadaña, *a feature reflected in the facade of Rancho dos Vidas.*

Spanish builders in the Southwest perfected the art of adobe masonry, building walls of adobe mud for protection and to keep the interiors cool in the parched climate. Fired red clay mission tiles covered the roofs.

Rancho dos Vidas is a compound set on top of a hill, its thick stucco walls stained to match the color of the surrounding red clay earth. Low snake walls buttress the house against the slope of the hillside.

(opposite page) Michael Imber has adopted the architecture of San Antonio's missions for this new hacienda in the hardscrabble Texas outback. The square tower of the guest bedroom wing is flanked by arcades of stucco beneath roofs of red mission tiles.

Designed like an old Spanish mission compound, the new house is a string of building parts clustered together into a protective enclosure. Whereas a mission would have had a church surrounded by a rectory, bedrooms, workshops, stables, and storehouses, Rancho dos Vidas is a compound of living rooms, bedrooms, kitchen, and garage connected together to form a courtyard enclosed within high walls.

Spanish courtyard at trail's end

At the end of a long gravel drive cut through scrubland, the house sits on a landscaped rise behind tall enclosing walls that hold the house on a hill. The entrance is guarded by a pair of sturdy wooden gates crafted like a Spanish *zaguán* that stands as an imposing entryway to the grounds. Behind the fortresslike walls, a raked-gravel courtyard forms a small plaza, the central feature around which a Spanish hacienda was planned. The courtyard is the heart of the house, a place of welcome civilization in the wilds.

The main facade of the house is sculpted like an *espadaña*, the belfry of a Spanish mission church. The front re-creates the unmistakable profile of churches such as Mission San Francisco de la Espada from which Imber derived the design. Typical of an espadaña, the front gable is tiered in stepped curves with a bell suspended within a pierced wall. The front door is a brawny oak portal and half-round transom window that form a majestic archway into the interior. This grand entrance has an old-world feeling, as if Zorro might come galloping through at any moment.

For centuries, the searing sun of the Southwest has driven architectural design. Imber designed the south-facing walls of the new house behind sturdy rows of Spanish arches, creating covered porches called *corredors*. Stretched across the southern and western flanks of the house, these deep porches shade the interiors by tempering the heat of the sun. The corredor roofs are covered with barrel-shaped mission tiles in

rich, earthen colors ranging from cream to ochre brown to terra-cottta.

Covered patios, courtyard gardens, and fountains are also a direct response to the sun-baked climate, time-honored traditions providing places of pleasure and relief. On the west-facing side of the house, Imber has created an intimate patio garden with a water fountain in the middle shaded by a bastionlike guest-house. This garden, just off the kitchen, is a cool

retreat beneath wooden arbors draped in flowering vines, a lush oasis carved out of the torrid Texas outback.

Baronial proportions

The grand front doorway opens into a cavernous vestibule like the foyer of a Spanish mission church. Seen through a tall arch, the living room is outsized and imposing, anchored by a cut-stone hearth at its far end. Imber conceived the room's tall proportions to be like the sanctuary of a church, with the fireplace taking the altar's place, under a high ceiling of wooden roof beams. From the entrance vestibule, a long hallway of arches marches off to other rooms of the house, repeating the arched pattern of the exterior corridors. An archway located

A pair of hefty raised-panel doors nearly 10 ft. tall swing open into a cavernous entry foyer. The doors have been worked by hand to appear weather-beaten with rusted wrought-iron door pulls and strap hinges for hardware.

(opposite page) The main facade of the house is sculpted like an espadaña—the belfry gable of a Spanish mission. Cut into the facade is a monumental archway for the front door that resembles the portal of a mission church.

TELLING DETAIL

ZAGUÁN

A *zaguán* is an entry gate built wide enough for large wagons to enter the courtyard of a ranch house, often with a smaller door set within the *zaguán* for pedestrian access. Inside the massive wooden gate was a large plaza, an enclosed patio garden, living quarters for the household and its servants, stables for animals, and storage buildings.

midway down the hall opens into the dining room. Surrounded on two sides by French doors, the room's Spanish reproduction furnishings, heavy damask drapes, and wrought-iron chandelier cast a baronial spell.

Down another hallway, the master bedroom fills the other end of the house. Its bright white walls are rough-cast plaster painted to look old and mottled, beneath a checkerboard pattern of wooden beams that crisscross the ceiling. A simple fireplace made of stucco and stone stands against the far wall, rising to the ceiling in supple Spanish curves.

Quintessentially Spanish Revival, the kitchen is a theater of colorful tile and stone set with Mexican crockery and ironwork. The center island rests on a pedestal of cream and celery glazed tiles, while the stained concrete floors are scored to look like square Saltillo tile pavers. Morning sunlight pours into the room through an ogee curve of windows, projecting a picture-postcard image of Old Spain.

BUILDING MISSIONS IN THE WILDERNESS

Throughout his new hacienda, Imber has used Spanish Colonial traditions to recall the story of the Spanish missions. Texas's missions were a complete Spanish settlement on the frontier, with a cadre of friars, soldiers, settlers, and natives governed by detailed Spanish laws. Franciscan friars and Spanish civilian governors created an urban villa around the mission church walled in by rooms that enclosed a central plaza. A small band of soldiers lived in barracks at a fortified presidio nearby.

In the rich farmland surrounding the villa, Spanish settlers cultivated farms that stretched for miles beyond the church, as well as cattle ranches to feed the mission villagers. They raised sheep, goats, and cows, forging the Texas cattle industry in the process. Meanwhile, the friars tended fruit orchards and vegetable gardens just outside the mission walls, while Indians cultivated maize, beans, and squash farther away.

The Indians were housed as neophytes in their own pueblo, a compact village of adobe huts adjacent to the mission grounds. Inside the villa, Indians were trained in the trades of weaving, ironwork, and carpentry needed to maintain the mission community. They provided the labor to build everything, including buildings, an activity that fostered a sense of community and a way to train native artisans.

The Spanish missions of New Spain were elaborately carved and decorated in a Baroque style known as Plateresque. *On the frontier, however, the lack of skilled Spanish masons meant that mission church designs had to be simplified for untrained Indian hands.*

(opposite page) Covered corridors *run along the southern and western sides of the house where exposure to the sun is greatest. Supported by continuous rows of arches,* corridors *were the principal shading device used in Spanish mission building.*

Seen through a tall archway, the dining room is baronial in scale. Created by interior designer Renee Green, the room features weighty period furnishings and damask drapes hung beneath a ceiling of wooden beams that recall the aura of Old Spain.

With clay plentiful in the San Antonio River Valley, adobe was the building material of choice. The friars taught the Indians to replace their traditional *jacals* of mud-covered sticks with houses made of sun-baked adobe bricks. They also taught them how to build in stone, constructing mission churches such as the Alamo from soft, yellow Texas limestone. Early mission roofs were thatched with reeds and grasses, but the flammable roofs were soon replaced by clay tiles baked on site.

Five missions of San Antonio

San Antonio boasts one of the greatest concentrations of Spanish missions in North America, five missions arrayed in a chain that follows the San Antonio River south for 10 miles. They were built close together for protection against Apache and Comanche Indian attacks and to share a common irrigation system. Three of the missions originally founded in East Texas as a buffer against the French were relocated to San Antonio.

The southernmost in the chain and most austere is Mission San Francisco de la Espada. Espada's sober facade resembles a giant tombstone made of rough Texas rubble stone mortared together with lime. The top of the wall is a tiered espadaña with bells suspended in three cutout arches, the architectural inspiration for the facade of Rancho dos Vidas.

The stone church and friary at Mission San Juan de Capistrano were completed in 1756. Made of limestone

(far left) The roughcast textured walls and rugged wooden ceiling beams of the master bedroom create a convincing patina of age.

(left) A confection of colorful Mexican tiles and wrought iron, the kitchen captures the spirit of the Spanish Colonial Revival of the 1920s.

rubble, San Juan's walls are a series of arches reinforced by stone buttresses that provide structure as well as decoration. This simple Spanish arcade is often repeated in Imber's design.

Mission San José y San Miguel de Aquayo, known as the "Queen of the Missions," was founded soon after the Alamo. In its heyday, San José was a community of 300 Indian neophytes and the major social and cultural center of San Antonio. The church is a classic cross in plan, with a dome over the crossing like the Renaissance cathedrals of Europe. Its elaborate frontispiece is a 16th-century Spanish design dripping with ornament and carved figures of the saints executed by sculptors from Mexico City.

The handsome stone church of Mission Nuestra Señora de La Purisima Concepción de Acuña is the least restored of San Antonio's missions. Its twin towers and belfries mix Renaissance arches with a Romanesque front portico. In its prime, the church walls were covered in geometric frescoes painted in yellow and orange squares and red and blue quatrefoils, but the patterns have long since faded.

MEXICAN JACAL

A *jacal* is a wattle-and-daub house built of closely spaced upright poles driven into the ground with a mat of small branches (wattle) interwoven between them. The mat is covered with adobe clay (daub) and lime plastered for additional weather protection. The *jacal's* flat roof of horizontal logs is covered with thatching, sometimes with a layer of adobe clay on top.

Mission Indians were housed in a pueblo village that was part of the mission grounds. Their primitive huts were made of rough stone or adobe walls with roofs covered in thatch or split shingles.

FLOWERING OF THE SPANISH MISSION REVIVAL

Secularized and abandoned by the Catholic Church in the 1790s, the Spanish missions fell into obscurity until the Panama–California Exposition of 1915 in San Diego. There, the grounds of Balboa Park sprouted inventive interpretations of Old Spain, Mexico, and the California missions, sowing the seeds of a revival. As the centerpiece of the fair, the California Building drew admiring eyes to the Spanish Colonial style.

Architect Bertram Grosvenor Goodhue's (1869–1924) design for this cathedral of white stucco and colored tile roofs awakened America to its Spanish roots at a time when Georgian architecture was considered the only proper colonial style. For the first time, the splendid mission churches of Mexico, California, Arizona, and Texas suggested a new style that could be adapted to houses, and so the Spanish Mission Revival was born.

(above) Mission San Francisco de la Espada.

(far left) Mission San Juan de Capistrano.

(left) The plentiful clay in the San Antonio River Valley provided material for building thick walls of adobe bricks covered in mud. Clay was also used to make half-round mission tiles that were formed over wooden molds and fired on site.

Mission San José y San Miguel de Aquayo.

(left) Architect Bertram Grosvenor Goodhue's California Building at the Panama–California Exposition (1915) dazzled the American public with visions of Spain, Mexico, and the Spanish missions, promoting a revival of the Spanish Mission style across the country.

This popular style of picturesque facades, irregular floor plans, plastered arches, and tile roofs appeared across suburban America in places far from the early Spanish colonies. By the 1920s when mail-order catalogs of house plans proliferated, designs for Spanish Colonial homes held a stature equal to the more established styles of early America.

San Antonio had its own champion of the Spanish Revival in architect Atlee B. Ayres (1873–1969), who documented the colonial architecture of Mexico in his 1926 book, *Mexican Architecture: Domestic, Civil, and Ecclesiastical.* Like all revival architects of the 1920s, his Spanish designs were a loose mixture of Mediterranean and Spanish Colonial details. Ayres and his son Robert designed many of the deftly detailed Spanish homes still prized in the San Antonio neighborhoods of Alamo Heights and Olmos Park, including the D. T. Atkinson House (1927), now the Marion Koogler McNay Art Museum.

Mission Nuestra Señora de La Purisima Concepción de Acuña.

Designed by Atlee B. Ayres in 1927, the Marion Koogler McNay Art Museum showcases the skillful interpretation of Spanish Mission architecture in the hands of San Antonio's most talented 20th-century revivalist.

(opposite page) Arcades of stucco-covered arches were used to construct the sheltering corridors of Spanish missions, a simple shading device repeated in Michael Imber's design.

Spanish Colonial Revival

"There never was a more peaceful or happy people on the face of the earth than the Spanish, Mexican, and Indian population of Alta California before the American conquest . . . Spanish Californians still tend to keep alive a spirit of love for the simple, homely, outdoor life of our Spanish ancestors on this coast . . . since the days when Father Junipero Serra planted the cross at Monterey."
—GUADALUPE VALLEJO, "Ranch and Mission Days in Alta California," *Century Magazine* (1890)

Los Angeles was once a sleepy 18th-century pueblo along the Spanish mission trail of Alta California, the region the Spanish called Upper California, as distinct from Baja or Lower California. Today, its Spanish colonial past is nearly invisible amid the sprawl of the modern City of Angels. Yet Spanish imagery adorns every corner of the city, a rebirth that began with the Spanish Colonial Revival of the 1920s.

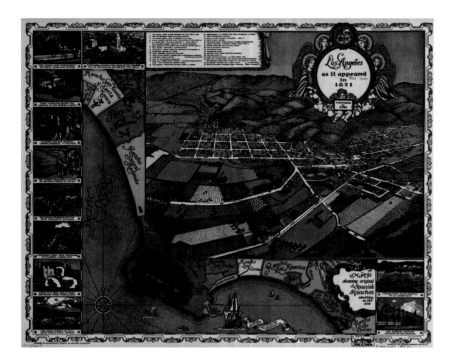

In the late 18th century, the City of Angels was a small pueblo village bordered by vast Spanish ranchos that sprawled down to the sea. In the next hundred years, the modern city began to take shape.

that pays homage to California's 18th-century heritage. Neff's original design reveals that in the past even an architect to the stars could build a house with authentic roots.

Now architect Steven Giannetti has restored the Neff House and added a suite of additions to complement the original architect's design. Just as Neff drew inspiration from California's early Spanish roots, so too does Giannetti from the Spanish Colonial Revival. His deference to tradition coupled with an equal measure of originality shows us the essence of a new old house—creating an authentic original.

Architect Wallace Neff (1895–1982) was a master of the Spanish style with a carriage-trade clientele of early Hollywood stars such as Douglas Fairbanks and Mary Pickford. In 1927 Neff designed one of his trademark Spanish Colonial Revival homes in West Hollywood

TRADITIONS OF MEXICO AND SPAIN

Spain established missions in California in a last ambitious attempt to extend its empire in the New World.

Steven Giannetti designed this new guesthouse in the spirit of the Spanish casas of early California. Its textured stucco walls, red mission tile roof, and suspended second-story balcony are telltale features of the style.

The 18th-century Spanish missions of California were designed as simple sheds beneath tile roofs with few ornamental details. Set off in the landscape by a bell tower, mission buildings were interconnected and sheltered from the sun by long arcades.

Casa California Plan

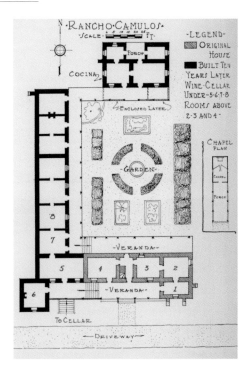

In a classic California Spanish Colonial casa, the house encloses an interior courtyard shaped by high walls and building parts to create a private patio, lined by covered corredors for circulation and shade. The plan of Rancho Camulos (1859) is an early single-story Spanish casa with corredors on three sides surrounding an interior plaza.

The adobe brick walls of the Jose Castro Adobe (1840s) were plastered with layers of mud and coated with white lime-wash. A classic Spanish Colonial wooden balcony was attached as an outdoor hallway to connect second-floor rooms.

From 1769 to 1791 Franciscan friars trudged up the California coast from San Diego to Sonoma, founding 21 missions along the way, including the chapel of Nuestra Señora de los Angeles in 1781. These missions and their attached pueblos of Indian converts formed small agricultural villages where the friars directed the spiritual, domestic, and working lives of the natives.

California's early mission architecture and dwellings were influenced by the building traditions of Mexico as much as by those of Spain. By the time missionaries reached California, the Spanish had been building in the New World for almost three centuries. Mexico City was the wealthy, urbane capital of New Spain, and Santa Fe, the provincial seat of New Mexico, was already 150 years old.

Attuned to the climate and resources of the Pacific Coast, California's missions were markedly different from those of Texas. With little building stone available, the friars depended on walls of adobe covered with mud plaster for their churches. The chapels were simple decorated sheds built behind an espadaña and bell tower, with few carved Renaissance details. Long arcades attached to the church walls sheltered rectories, workrooms, living spaces, and stables from California's searing sun.

Homebuilding in early California was a stripped-down version of Mexican construction. Dependent on primitive Indian building skills, the first homes were jacals made of posts set in the ground, bound together with willow branches, and covered by thatched roofs. In Mexico, Spaniards had been building with adobe bricks, cut stone, and fired clay tiles for centuries. Soon the friars introduced adobe construction techniques in California, to which they added wooden balconies, carved woodwork, and wrought-iron grilles.

The earliest adobe houses were modeled after the farmhouses of the Mexican countryside. They were shaped around an interior courtyard that was screened from public view by high walls and surrounded on three sides by long strings of rooms. The most important rooms opened directly onto the courtyard under covered corridors, supported by continuous arcades of columns and arches. Adobe walls were stuccoed with lime-and-sand mortar, and then, year after year, painted with whitewash to form a bright and durable exterior skin.

Architect Wallace Neff, a master of the 1920s Spanish Colonial Revival, drew his inspiration from Mexican farmhouses, Spanish missions, and the historic adobe houses of Monterey.

(opposite page) Inspired by the provincial farmhouses of southern Spain, the art studio wraps around a square tower with a window balcony cantilevered off the wall. The balcony rests on a string of beams with teardrop-carved ends.

In the Style of Wallace Neff

Visions of whitewashed Mexican farmhouses, California missions, and Monterey's adobe casas inspired the design of Steven Giannetti's additions to the Neff house. Fortune had smiled on the owner of the original house when he was able to purchase the lot next door. He wanted to create a classic Spanish hacienda, a small village of buildings enclosed within high walls of hedgerows and stucco piers. Working with the strong bones of the 1920s original, Giannetti added a guesthouse, art studio, and greenhouse arranged around a courtyard garden.

Neff's original design displays the essential ingredients of the Spanish Colonial Revival style: plain walls of white stucco, roofs of red mission tiles, arched windows and doors, overhanging balconies, and wrought-iron decorative details. Giannetti studied this palette thoroughly. The new guesthouse is a boxy rectangle of spare

Concealed behind a wall of hedgerows and stucco piers, the new guesthouse rises above the wall to mark one corner of the inner courtyard garden, a contemporary take on a traditional Spanish courtyard design.

TELLING DETAIL

LEGACY OF THE MOORS

The exotic bay window is a legacy of the Moors, who occupied Spain's Iberian Peninsula for three centuries before Columbus. Spanish architecture was strongly influenced by Moorish details, with pointed arches, domes, water gardens, and decorative ornaments becoming a permanent part of Spanish design and, later, the Spanish Colonial Revival in Southern California.

The intimate patio garden off the guesthouse is a private retreat beneath a vine-covered arbor. The outdoor fireplace flanked by tiled bancos, *or seating benches, makes sense in California's balmy climate, where outdoor living is a revered tradition.*

white stucco walls, frameless windows and doors, and a red tile roof that sits low and snug on top of the house. Adorning the simple structure are decorative details from the Spanish Colonial tradition: an arched stairway, a bay window, and a second-floor balcony.

In the 1920s, the charming spectacle of a porch dangling in the air was an irresistible detail that architects used to capture the spirit of Old California. Visible from the street, the balcony on the new guesthouse is the most captivating feature of Giannetti's additions. It is a high perch suspended in air on heavy beams in classic Monterey style. The slender, turned wooden columns supporting the tile roof are somewhat fancier than their historic precedents in Monterey and are closer to the typical porch posts of French Colonial Louisiana.

For the playful bay window on the guesthouse, Giannetti looked again to Neff for guidance. The bay is a replica of one Neff designed on the original house.

From a distance it looks like a crenellated king's crown that has ended up on the house by mistake. The bay is made of wooden panels and mouldings painted dark green, its facets framed by tall, round posts with finials on top that resemble giant chess pawns.

Like the guesthouse, the art studio has plain stucco walls and its own distinctive Spanish features. A short, square tower stands at its most visible corner like a defensive lookout from provincial Andalusia. Next to the tower is a window balcony cantilevered off the wall on a string of hefty beams, their decorative ends carved into a row of teardrops. Outdoor stairs rise up to meet the balcony, the steps faced with painted terra-cotta tiles reminiscent of the festive stairways of Mexico and Spain.

The sunroom is a light-filled wall of glass doors fit into wide, round arches. The ceiling is bowed to reflect the shape of the arches, creating a sculptural white canopy that bounces light across the tiled floor.

(left) The foyer floor is a checkerboard pattern of mahogany-and-white marble. Neff designed the elegant floating staircase with a sinuous handrail of vines rather than a traditional row of pickets, a theme that appears again in the front door.

Decorative painted tile risers and terracotta treads traced by an iron handrail enrich the stairway to the art studio, a common sight on the patio houses of old Mexico.

(above) "Bottle glass" takes its name from the center cores of cylinder glass, made by spinning a ball of molten glass into a flat plate from which to cut window panes. The leftover cores were traditionally used for decorative windows such as fanlights and sidelights.

(right) The Moorish-inspired bay window of the guesthouse cuts into the living room wall beneath a ceiling of new hand-hewn beams. Round glass cylinders that resemble the bottoms of wine bottles fill the lower panes of the leaded-glass windows.

Casa de la Guerra, Santa Barbara.

Mixing history

The architects of the Spanish Colonial Revival were eclectic in their use of history. They would pick and choose themes to fit their designs, often mixing elements from Italy, France, and England into a free interpretation of Spanish. This loose invention with tradition showed up most often in the interiors of their houses, and Neff was no exception. The entrance hall to his West Hollywood house is more French than Spanish—an oval-shaped foyer from a French *hotel de ville* unexpectedly inserted into a Spanish floor plan.

Architect Giannetti had a field day designing a new kitchen for the Neff House. The ceiling is a riot of colored tiles set into a grid of wooden beams. An inventive allusion to Spanish mural painting, the design shows us how today's new old house architects extend tradition by breaking the rules. The glass wall cabinets are transparent front and back, and though they cover the windows, allow sunlight to pour into the kitchen.

The most intriguing feature inside the guesthouse is the bay window, which looks Moorish from the outside and like a tapestry of glass from the inside. Each win-

Casa Bonifacio, Monterey.

Interior courtyard of Wallace Neff House, West Hollywood.

dow pane is leaded glass and full of air bubbles, ripples, and stray lines that shimmer and distort the view. In the trade this type of glass is called "seedy glass" because of its artful imperfections. Round cylinders of "bottle glass"—resembling the bottoms of wine bottles—fill the bottom pane of each window.

ADOBES OF SOUTHERN CALIFORNIA

Like Neff before him, Giannetti borrowed freely from the Spanish past for his design, and he had plenty of examples to study. California is a treasury of preserved missions and adobe houses, from San Diego to Santa Barbara and Monterey.

Casa de la Guerra (1819–27) is a classic Spanish courtyard house in the heart of Santa Barbara. Probably built by Indian hands for Jose de la Guerra, the commandant of the Santa Barbara Presidio, its adobe brick walls are 3½ ft. thick, plastered inside and out, and coated with whitewash. In a region prone to earthquakes, most early adobes had thick walls to resist shaking ground and to carry heavy roof beams.

Built in Monterey, Casa Bonifacio (1835) was moved and restored on a new site in 1922 by California landscape painter Percy Gray. Reconstructed brick by

Thomas Larkin House, Monterey (1835).

brick, this adobe casa reflects the liberties taken with historic houses in the 1920s, for it is more Spanish Colonial Revival than provincial Californian. Telling details include a second-floor balcony resting on cantilevered floor beams and picturesque tile-roofed additions that lean against the walls.

The classic Monterey street balcony made its first appearance on the house built by Thomas Oliver Larkin in 1835. A merchant from Massachusetts, Larkin designed his adobe house in the Spanish Colonial style, with adobe bricks measuring 4 in. by 12 in. by 24 in. long. He may have modeled his second-floor balcony after those he had seen while trading in the West Indies. Balconies soon became a popular custom throughout Monterey.

Probably inspired by Larkin's design, Spaniard Don Jose Amesti added in 1855 a second story with a projecting balcony across the front of his adobe house of 1834. He did away with first-floor support posts in favor of suspending his balcony on second-floor beams cantilevered out over the wall. From then on, street balconies were everywhere in town and eventually inspired the trademark detail of mid-20th-century California ranch houses.

REINVENTING SPANISH STYLE

American veterans returning from World War I were captivated by the architecture they had seen in Europe, and in California this fascination spurred a revival of the state's Spanish Colonial architecture. Spanish Colonial was only one of many historic European styles that were used for modern homes in this first wave of

Casa Amesti, Monterey (1834).

Although a 20th-century revival design, the layout of Tao House (1937), by architect Fredrick Confer, shows the classic plan of a Spanish Colonial casa, with walls that enclose an interior courtyard, creating a private patio lined by covered corredors for circulation and shade.

CALIFORNIA RANCH HOUSE

The California ranch house of the 1950s represented an updated version of a traditional Spanish *rancho,* creating a home for modern living adapted to California's benign climate. Invented by architect Cliff May (1908–89) in 1931 as the "Western ranch house," the home featured an open, single-level floor plan that was shaped around a patio garden and set low to the ground beneath a shallow overhanging roof. Walls of glass brought outdoor living inside, drawing sunlight, views, and cross ventilation. Casual, informal, and innovative, its design captured the relaxed sensibility of the postwar era and was relentlessly promoted by *Sunset* magazine as the new American ideal, catching on in suburbs across the country.

new old houses. Architects and builders were quick to pick up on the popular taste for European styles, and new suburban neighborhoods across the country soon sprouted Mediterranean villas, English Tudor cottages, and French chateaus.

Architects of the 1920s Spanish Colonial Revival learned most of what they knew from books of photographs and measured drawings showing historic Spanish buildings, among them *Provincial Houses in Spain* by antiquarians Arthur Byne and Mildred Stapley, and *Early Mexican Houses* by architects Richard Garrison and George Rustay. Studying these folios, architects could teach themselves about authentic details without having visited them.

Spanish Colonial designs were interpretive, not literal. They mixed details from the houses of Spain, Italy, and Mexico in a romantic Mediterranean style, with a dollop of Spanish mission and California casa thrown in. Walls of roughcast white stucco, red mission tile roofs, arched windows, cantilevered balconies, and fancy ironwork became hallmarks of the Spanish Colonial Revival. The style was most popular in California and Florida, where architects such as George Washington Smith (1876–1930) and Addison Mizner (1872–1933) transformed the cityscapes of Santa Barbara and Palm Beach in the image of Old Spain.

RANCHO DON RAIMUNDO OLIVAS

In 1841 Don Raimundo Olivas received nearly 5,000 acres that were originally part of Mission San Buenaventura in Ventura as payment for his loyal military service to the Mexican Republic. Olivas began raising cattle on his ranch in 1847, just as gold was discovered in California. He soon prospered by selling livestock to feed hungry prospectors.

His first house was a small adobe. As the Olivas family grew, he added a two-story ranch house completed in 1852. Rancho Olivas is a classic California rancho built in the early American period, one of the few remaining survivors in Southern California. Still surrounded by open fields, the house is enclosed within high walls that form a protected courtyard. The courtyard is gated on the south side by a picturesque bell tower and its massive wooden zaguán.

The Olivas adobe blends details from Mexican and early Spanish architecture. Its walls are adobe bricks laid in mud mortar and plastered inside and out, covered by a roof of cedar shingles. Wooden balconies that hang off both sides of the house are a classic feature of Mexican colonial ranchos.

(far left) Facing south, the two-story balcony on Rancho Olivas provided a hallway to connect the long string of rooms, a place for outdoor relaxation and socializing, and covered shaded from the sun.

(left) The enclosed courtyard of Rancho Olivas was originally entered through this gateway cut through the high perimeter walls.

(opposite page) In a Spanish Colonial casa, the kitchen was a utilitarian room of bare necessities with whitewashed adobe walls and a hard-packed earthen floor where many of the indoor household chores were done.

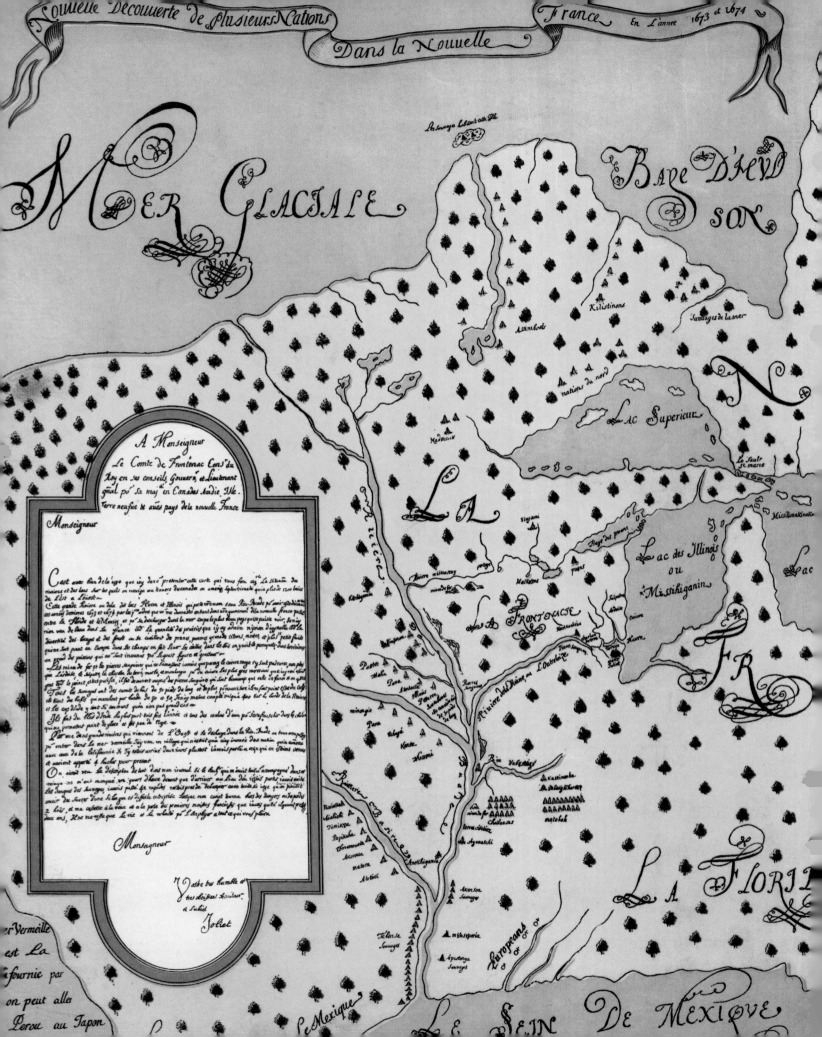

2

OUR FRENCH HERITAGE

RIVER ROADS, INDIAN ALLIES

"Hence 'twill be seen that this superiority of the French in America is in some sort accidental, and if they neglect to maintain it, whilst the English are making every effort to destroy it, 'twill pass into the hands of the latter. There is no doubt but such an event would be followed by the entire destruction of our settlements in that part of the Globe."

—ROLAND-MICHEL BARRIN DE LA GALISSONIÈRE,
Memoir on the French Colonies in North America (1750)

A s the Middle Ages drew to a close, Portugal, Spain, France, England, and the Netherlands were locked in a bitter rivalry to find a route west to Cathay and the Indies. The one who got there first would control the spice trade and with it the reins of power in Renaissance Europe. Discovering an easy water passage through America proved a fantasy, but the quest spurred centuries of exploration.

Although the French failed in their search for the mythical passage to the Orient, they found instead the bounties of the New World, discovering a rich source of commerce in furs, lumber, and minerals. Pushing deep into the interior, French frontiersmen established trading posts with the native Indians. By the 18th century, these scattered settlements had become the cities of Montreal, Quebec, Detroit, Duluth, St. Louis, and New Orleans. The period of French ascendancy ended in 1763 when their colonial empire collapsed after the French and Indian War and the British took control of French lands.

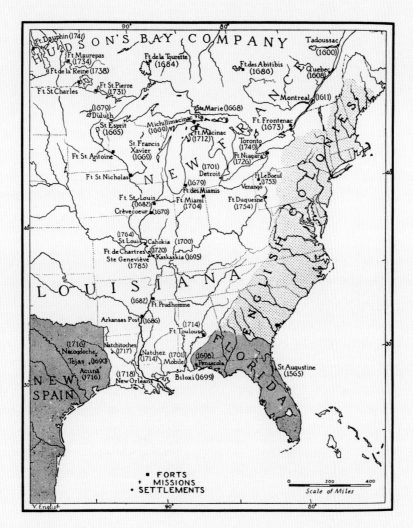

As the 17th century came to a close, New France controlled the heartland of the North American continent from the Great Lakes and Canada to the Mississippi Valley, effectively hemming in the British colonies on the Atlantic seaboard.

CHARTING THE AMERICAN FRONTIER

As early as 1534, French explorer Jacques Cartier followed the St. Lawrence River from Acadia (Nova Scotia) into Canada looking for the fabled route to the Indies. Samuel de Champlain pressed westward to the Great Lakes in 1607. Decades later, René-Robert Cavelier de La Salle, lured by Indian tales of a great continental river, followed the course of the Mississippi to its delta in 1682. Mapping everything he found, La Salle took French possession of the land he christened *La Louisiane* for King Louis XIV, including the entire Mississippi Valley and the Illinois Country bounded by the Ohio and Missouri rivers.

By the time of the French and Indian War, France had laid claim to an enormous territory covering all of Canada and Louisiana, effectively encircling the English on the Atlantic Coast and walling off New Spain to the south. But while England focused on sending shiploads of colonists to populate permanent settlements, France was unwilling to back up its land grab with settlers. French religious dissidents such as the Huguenots came to found new colonies but had no support from the crown. After nearly a century of trying to establish a foothold, fewer than 6,000 Frenchmen called America home.

Indian Furs and Palisade Walls

French settlements were widely scattered and sparsely populated. Strung out along the frontier, they served as outposts for defense, trade, and missionary work. Many towns started as forts under military control, among them Fort Niagara, Fort Duquesne, and Fort St. Louis. While soldiers provided security, French fur traders and merchants—*coureurs de bois*—bartered with the Iroquois, Algonquian, and Illinois Indians. Missionaries converted the natives to Catholicism and eagerly studied their languages, customs, and histories. Unlike the Spanish, the French forged alliances with the Indians, who served as allies, guides, trading partners, farmers, and even spouses in their effort to control a vast territory.

Many early French émigrés came from the Atlantic coast of France, where the longhouses of Normandy and Brittany had been built in much the same way since Roman times. The rural farmhouses were half-timbered, with the spaces between posts and beams filled in with stone or brick. When they settled in America, the French adapted this technique to climates as diverse as their territories were distant, from the frigid shores of the St. Lawrence River to the subtropical bayous of the Mississippi Delta.

In the early 1600s when the French first arrived in heavily wooded Acadia and Canada, they improvised shelter using logs to build walls of vertical posts set into trenches in the ground. These palisades of vertical logs were chinked with clay to make them weather-tight and planked with split-board roofs. Called *poteaux-en-terre* (posts-in-the-ground) construction, this wall-building technique was used throughout the Northwest Territory and Great Lakes to build forts, churches, and stores as well as homes.

The traditional farmhouses of French Normandy were called longhouses, made of timber post-and-beam frames infilled with small stones or bricks. Covered by a steeply pitched roof hipped at both ends, the Normandy longhouse was adapted for French settlements in the St. Lawrence River Valley.

As French settlers spread into the North American interior, they built houses of posts driven into the ground called poteaux-en-terre. *The walls were chinked with clay and later sided with clapboards beneath a steep, overhanging roof of shingles.*

Creole cottages in the Mississippi Delta married traditions from New France and the French West Indies in homes built with cypress timber frames raised aboveground on piers. The spaces between timbers were filled with an adobe-like paste of clay and moss called bousillage.

CREOLES AND CAJUNS

Toward the end of the 17th century, the French arrived in the Lower Mississippi Valley. The hot and humid climate, prone to seasonal flooding and hurricanes, was very different from what they had known in the forests of the North. To suit these new conditions, French settlers merged the cold-climate building traditions of New France with those of the French West Indies, creating Creole- and Cajun-style homes.

Designed for the subtropical climate, Creole houses were built of cypress timbers pegged together into rigid frames and raised aboveground on piers—a throwback to the half-timbered houses of France. Their open web of timbers was filled in with *bousillage,* a thick mat of clay and moss, and then coated with lime plaster. Under a pavilion roof—a tentlike form that had been developed in the Caribbean—deep porches surrounded the house on all four sides, providing shelter from the sun and capturing cooling breezes.

Cajun cottages—a colloquial corruption of Acadian—were also timber frames filled with bousillage and covered with cypress boards, but their roofs were a simple gable of saltbox shape that included a front porch. The style was adapted from the early houses

of Acadia and brought to the Gulf Coast by French refugees expelled from that colony by the British in 1755 to 1763.

Meanwhile, Creole townhouses in 18th-century New Orleans were built of timbers and *briquette-entre-poteaux* (bricks-between-posts) construction, such as Madame John's Legacy and Lafitte's Blacksmith Shop. This building style largely defined the architecture of the Crescent City until President Thomas Jefferson purchased Louisiana in 1803. Sadly, much of early French Colonial architecture outside of Louisiana has not survived the rapacious march of progress, save for a few well-preserved homes in towns such as Ste. Genevieve, Missouri.

FRENCH CREOLE COTTAGE

"The Mississippi River towns are comely, clean, well built, and pleasing to the eye, and cheering to the spirit. The Mississippi Valley is as reposeful as dreamland, nothing worldly about it…nothing to hang a fret or worry upon."
—MARK TWAIN, *Life on the Mississippi* (1863)

Thomas Jefferson's purchase of the Louisiana Territory from Napoleon in 1803 is one of the great triumphs of American history. The Louisiana Purchase doubled the size of the New Republic and annexed all that remained of France's colonial dominions in the continental United States. With this prize came control of the Mississippi Valley and the cosmopolitan city of New Orleans, a melting pot of cultures from around the globe.

Across Lake Pontchartrain from New Orleans, along the banks of the Tchefuncte River, sits the old Creole town of Madisonville. There, restoration builder Ron Arnoult has re-created a traditional Creole cottage with roots in French Colonial architecture. Its half-timbered walls resemble the medieval houses of Normandy that inspired French colonists who settled in Canada. Blending the timber frame with *galerie* porches and a pavilion roof derived from the plantation houses of the French West Indies, Arnoult has revived all the hallmarks of the classic Creole cottage.

CREOLES AND CAJUNS ON THE RIVER

In the 17th century, the Louisiana Territory covered the vast heartland of the American continent, held by France in isolated forts and trading posts scattered throughout the wilderness. In the wake of French

The territory the French called La Louisiane *encompassed the entire Mississippi River basin, including the Ohio and Missouri river valleys, and reached from the Appalachian Mountains to the western plains.*

(opposite page) This Creole cottage re-created by Ron Arnoult in Madisonville, Louisiana, is a reprise of the classic hipped pavilion roof and gallery porches that defined the raised cottages of the French colonial era.

FRENCH TIMBER-POST CONSTRUCTION

Many early Creole houses were made of heavy timber posts set upright in the ground, a primitive form of log construction called *poteaux-en-terre.* The spaces between posts were filled with *bousillage,* a mixture of clay, lime, and Spanish moss, and covered with a protective layer of stucco or weatherboards. When an infill of soft brick nogging was used it was known as *briquette-entre-poteaux.* In *poteaux-sur-sole* construction, vertical posts were mounted on a wooden sill, forming a timber frame that was raised aboveground on stone or brick piers, a style known as the Creole "raised cottage."

explorers, soldiers and traders followed the Mississippi south from the Great Lakes to the Gulf, creating sparsely settled colonial outposts all along the way. Duluth was founded in 1679, then Cahokia near St. Louis in 1699, followed by Natchez in 1714, and the capital of New Orleans in 1718.

During the 18th century, the Mississippi Valley between St. Louis and New Orleans was alternately controlled by France and Spain before being purchased by Jefferson in 1803. The valley became home to a cross section of old-world cultures that bred an unusual architectural tradition known as Creole, meaning of mixed European ancestry.

French Acadians (Cajuns) heading down the river encountered French, Spanish, and African émigrés (Creoles) from Haiti and Cuba paddling north. As they mingled and traded in the river towns, over decades their architectural traditions merged in designs for cottages, plantations, and townhouses suited to the climate of the bayou country.

The hybrid Creole cottage is a perfect marriage between the half-timbered houses of French Canada and the deep covered porches of West Indies plantation houses. From Canada came the pavilion roof and half-timbered structural frame, both with origins in the traditional longhouses of Normandy. Creoles from the West Indies contributed the shaded gallery porches, stucco walls, and raised foundation piers that are trademarks of Creole cottage design.

TELLING DETAIL

PAVILION ROOF

The steep, hipped pavilion roof looks like a pyramid stretched out along the length of the house, a shape unique to French Colonial architecture. The roof is "hipped" because all four sides are sloped at a steep angle, unlike a gable roof, which has only two sloped sides.

Seventeenth-century French houses in the Mississippi Valley blended traditions from French Canada and the West Indies. The hybrid house had timberframe walls built up on raised foundations, covered by a pavilion roof with gallery porches surrounding four sides.

(opposite page) The gallery porch of the new old house is an outdoor living room that opens to the house through French doors. Its timber ceiling is painted gros rouge, *also called Spanish Brown, a classic Louisiana colonial paint color.*

Classic Creole Roots

Arnoult calls the raised Creole cottage he has re-created in Madisonville the Cemetery House because it is across the street from the town's oldest cemetery grounds. Sitting on a quiet corner where the neighbors don't say a word, the house recalls the architecture that Arnoult has known all his life. He was born into an old New Orleans family with Creole culture in its blood.

Before he began building the new house, Arnoult did his homework. He went on a refresher tour to study historic details, traveling through old towns along the Mississippi from Ste. Genevieve, Missouri, to St. Francisville, Louisiana. With camera and measuring tape in hand, he cataloged the telling details of classic Creole cottages.

Cemetery House captures the true spirit of a raised cottage in its gallery porches and hipped roof. It is a single story tall and appears low and long, even though it is lifted several feet above the ground on masonry piers. Raised foundations were a customary architectural detail on early Creole cottages, allowing air to circulate under the house to keep it cool and to prevent moisture from rotting the floor timbers.

An umbrella over the porch

A tall, hipped pavilion roof, known locally as an "umbrella roof," dominates the appearance of the house from the street. Thought to derive from the houses of French Normandy, the pavilion roof found its way to Louisiana via Canada. In the Mississippi Valley, the Normandy roof merged with the West Indies tradition of shallow roofs covering gallery porches, creating a unique roof that breaks in two distinct pitches. Pavilion roofs grace plantation houses all along Louisiana's River Road.

A half-dozen stairs climb up to the front porch of Cemetery House. Known in French as a *galerie,* the gallery porch runs the whole length of the facade, tucked under the roof and supported by simple posts called *colonnettes.* Before there was air-conditioning, the gallery was a necessity in sultry Louisiana as an outdoor sitting room. It was where you got out of the sun at noon, chatted with the neighbors in the evening, and sipped mint juleps after dark.

French doors open onto the gallery porch from the front parlors. These doors are old salvaged pairs that Arnoult collected in his years as a restoration builder in New Orleans. Made of cypress wood, the door panels are weathered and scarred with a rough patina of age that only nature can produce. The window panes are old crown glass with surface ripples and tiny air pockets typical of early 19th-century glass making.

The stucco walls of Cemetery House, painted French yellow ochre, are set within a timber frame. Although the

→ WORDSMITH ←

• bousillage •

Bousillage describes an infill of loaves of clay mud caked by hand over a mat of sticks laced between timber posts. The *bousillage* is then covered with a finished coat of mud. After the mud dries, the walls are coated inside and out with limewash that hardens into a protective shell.

half-timbers are fake, they recall the way early Creole cottages were put together with heavy posts and beams. The wide gaps between timbers were filled in with bousillage to serve as infill, insulation, and finished wall surface.

Simple square posts called colonnettes *support the pavilion roof over the front porch. Known in French Colonial architecture as a* galerie, *the gallery porch is the distinctive feature of Creole cottage design.*

Salvaged French doors weathered by time add the patina of age, with much of their original glass and narrow wood muntins still intact. Antique box locks painted with a traditional coating of black asphalt are mounted on the face of the doors.

Pairs of board-and-batten shutters frame the doorway to the loggia *porch outside of the kitchen.*

Two small rooms called cabinets *filled the back corners of a Creole cottage. Used as storerooms or spare bedrooms for guests, the cabinets were accessible only from a covered back porch, or* loggia, *that ran between them.*

(opposite page) The interior walls and woodwork are painted in a traditional 18th-century French palette of earthy yellow ochre, mustard, and walnut brown.

Creole hall-and-parlor

At the back corners of a traditional Creole cottage, there were often two small rooms called *cabinets* used for spare bedrooms or storerooms. The cabinets opened onto a covered back porch running between them called a *loggia*. Back rooms were often added by enclosing gallery porches to make more interior living space. The back rooms of Cemetery House are sided with wood clapboards rather than stucco, imitating a Creole cottage that has changed over time.

Inside an early Creole cottage, the floor plan was called a *salle-chambre,* or hall-parlor, arranged in a row of two or three rooms that filled the front of the house. There was no real front door. Instead, pairs of French doors opened from the front parlors onto the gallery porch. Since there were no hallways in French Creole houses, the gallery became a passage between rooms.

(far left) Poche-Ezidore House, dating from the early 1800s, is a raised cottage in Gramercy, Louisiana, built of heavy timbers with bousillage *infill.*

(left) At Cemetery House, double parlors are joined together through a tall door frame and transom window. The doorway appears to hold a pair of sliding doors but is a clever bit of fakery: A single old door has been cut in half and set in the frame to look like a pair.

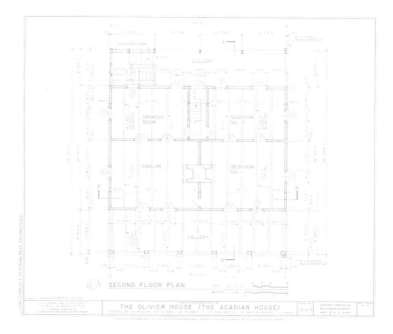

SECOND FLOOR PLAN

THE OLIVIER HOUSE (THE ACADIAN HOUSE)

The plan of a classic Creole cottage was a salle-chambre design arranged as a row of parlors and bedrooms opening directly onto the gallery porch through French doors. There were no interior hallways to impede the flow of cooling breezes. The back of the house opened to another gallery porch or was divided into two small cabinets with a loggia between them.

Arnoult's plan for Cemetery House rearranges the traditional plan to accommodate modern lifestyles but does so with few compromises. Two parlors and the master bedroom string together across the front, while the back has the kitchen in the middle instead of the traditional loggia. The master bathroom and guest bedroom are in the back corners where the cabinets would have been. The new arrangement is so simple that it makes the house live larger than its 2,300 sq. ft. while still preserving authentic Creole roots.

Creole ceilings were made 10 ft. tall or higher to draw hot air to the upper part of the room, a practical system of cooling in the days before air-conditioning. The tall ceilings of the new house are finished with wooden boards instead of drywall. Another old Creole tradition, ceilings were planked rather than plastered to resist damage from humidity, then painted in strong colors such as indigo, verdigris, and yellow ochre. Throughout Cemetery House, the walls and woodwork are earthy mineral colors, a traditional 18th-century French palette that reinforces the authenticity of this new old Creole cottage.

MISSISSIPPI RIVER TOWNS: STE. GENEVIEVE AND CAHOKIA

Cemetery House has forbearers in small towns scattered up and down the Mississippi. Beginning in the late 17th century, French Colonial houses were built all along the river from the Great Lakes to the Gulf of Mexico. Almost none of the earliest French houses survive, but a splendid collection of later vintage has been

The living room mantelpiece is an antique 19th-century Creole design with deep side panels. French Colonial mantels wrap around the chimney breast and touch the back wall, standing proud in the room like a piece of fine furniture.

preserved in the town of Ste. Genevieve, Missouri, which Arnoult toured in search of telling details. Founded on the river near present-day St. Louis in 1735, Ste. Genevieve's fertile bottomland became the breadbasket of the Mississippi Valley, supplemented by nearby salt springs and mineral deposits. The old trading town is now a living village of French Colonial architecture, with many of the restored homes still inhabited. Two outstanding landmarks are the Louis Bolduc House of 1785 and the Bequette-Ribault House of 1793.

Louis Bolduc was a Canadian fur trader who built his French Creole cottage out of squared timbers set into the ground. The timbers are spaced 6 in. apart and insulated with a filling of clay, manure, and horsehair finished with limewash. The high-peaked roof is framed of oak trusses pegged together in a technique reminiscent of medieval France. A pieux debout fence of pointed cypress planks surrounds the house as a stockade to keep animals in.

Authentic Creole details incorporated in the Cemetery House include a 19th-century Louisiana mantel with its cracked and chipped varnish carefully preserved.

The house of Frenchman Jean Baptiste Bequette is of classic poteaux-en-terre construction. Its vertical log walls are surrounded on four sides by gallery porches raised aboveground on porch posts—a practice the French adopted from the West Indies. Inside the long, rectangular one-story house are two rooms separated by a central stair up to the attic sleeping loft. A French-African, Clarise Ribault, purchased the building in the 1840s, making the Bequette-Ribault House the only home in Ste. Genevieve owned by a free woman of color.

The earliest permanent French settlement on the Mississippi River is the town of Cahokia, Illinois, founded in 1699. Originally the riverside summer camp of the Cahokia Indians, the village became home to both French and Indians who comfortably intermingled in trade, worship, and marriage. The poteaux-en-terre house built there by Jean Baptiste Saucier in 1737 was purchased in 1793 to be a county courthouse.

Now known as Cahokia Courthouse, it is the oldest surviving example of French pioneer log construction in the Mississippi Valley. Its log walls rest on stone foundations beneath a pavilion roof that extends over gallery porches. After being dismantled and moved to the Louisiana Purchase Exposition in St. Louis in 1904, the courthouse was rebuilt on its original site by the Works Progress Administration in 1938.

CREOLE RISING

Creole architecture runs deep in the hearts of Louisiana's native sons, among them Baton Rouge architect A. Hays Town (1903–2005). Carrying the vernacular tradition into the late 20th century, Town became syn-

onymous with elegantly crafted interpretations of the Creole style. His work blended a thorough knowledge of Louisiana's French, Spanish, and American precedents with an inventive use of salvaged timbers, antique bricks, and cypress paneling. Town's marriage of history with the necessities of modern living made him one of the early pioneers of the new old house.

Town mingled building details from West Indies plantations, Creole townhouses, and Acadian raised cottages into an architectural story with a unique personal signature. His homes were an elegant synthesis of Acadian raised porches, Spanish courtyards, and French doors with full-length shutters. Other trademarks included plantation outbuildings such as *pigeonniers* (a French pigeon roost), courtyard fountains, cypress paneling, and brick floors coated with beeswax. Almost every home built in Louisiana during the last 20 years has been inspired in some way by Town's work.

Bequette-Ribault House, Ste. Genevieve, Missouri (1793).

Baton Rouge architect A. Hays Town (1903–2005) perfected a signature style that blended the details of Creole cottages, New Orleans townhouses, and West Indies plantations in a rich brew of Louisiana's unique architectural traditions.

The restored Louis Bolduc House (1785) in Ste. Genevieve, Missouri, is a splendid survivor of early French Colonial homebuilding in the Mississippi Valley.

POCHE-EZIDORE HOUSE

There is an original Creole cottage from the early 1800s in the town of Gramercy, Louisiana, on the banks of the Mississippi River. Poche-Ezidore House is not widely known beyond Gramercy, but this primitive cottage has found a caretaker in Dr. Roy Boucvalt, who has preserved the house and others like it in his passion for French Louisiana history.

Poche-Ezidore House is a raised cottage built of heavy timbers with bousillage infill. Restored by Ron Arnoult, the house looks like a period timepiece. It is filled with antique furniture of museum quality but is nevertheless meant to be lived in, not merely admired.

The cottage seems unremarkable from the street, a simple box under a pavilion roof that stands on brick piers. Not until you climb the long flight of stairs to the gallery porch do you realize that this is no ordinary cottage. The front wall is made of cracked and crumbling bousillage framed between rustic cypress timbers. The wall was once covered by weatherboards but has been uncovered to showcase the original construction.

Inside, the house is two rooms deep with a parlor in front and a bedroom off to each side. Layers of paint have been left peeling off the plaster walls to reveal the original mineral paint colors, from Prussian blue to red oxide—a vestige of the past that the owner is happy to live with.

A single partition wall divides the floor plan in half, separating the front rooms from the back. The parlor opens through French doors into the dining room and then out to the back loggia. Doors line up through the middle of the house, drawing river breezes for natural ventilation. There is nothing pretentious about the kitchen, fitted out with 1940s porcelain metal cabinets and appliances as if the last owners just left six decades ago.

(top left) An early 19th-century Louisiana Creole cottage that survives on the banks of the Mississippi River, Poche-Ezidore House is of timber-frame construction with walls of bousillage raised up on brick piers.

(top center) The interior rooms have been lightly restored by repairing structural problems while leaving the original colors and loose layers of paint as reminders of the living legacy of the house.

(top right) On the front wall of the house, the bousillage infill between posts has been exposed by removing old weatherboards to show the original mud and moss construction.

(left) Set in the center of the house between the front parlor and back loggia, the dining room walls are painted in a Creole palette of earthy moss greens and furnished with museum-quality antiques as well as folk pieces.

FRENCH COLONIAL PLANTATION HOUSE

"From Baton Rouge to New Orleans, the great sugar plantations border both sides of the river all the way…standing so close together, for long distances, that the broad river lying between two rows becomes a sort of spacious street."
—MARK TWAIN, *Life on the Mississippi* (1863)

When Frenchman René-Robert Cavelier de La Salle sailed the Mississippi to its delta in 1682, he discovered what would become America's greatest inland waterway. Within a hundred years, the river's docks would be bustling with trade and its banks would be lined with prosperous sugar plantations generating enormous wealth. At the mouth of this river of commerce rose the city of New Orleans, a cosmopolitan world trading port with a distinctly old-world architectural character.

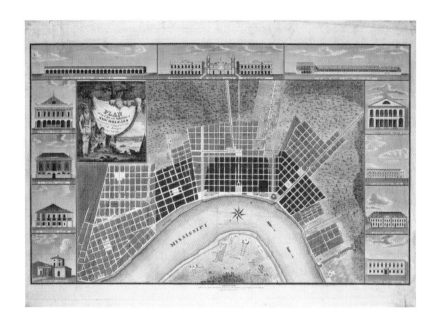

porches, it illustrates the unique blend of French and West Indies design influences that created the French Colonial plantations of Louisiana's River Road.

BUILDING THE RIVER ROAD

New Orleans and its River Road were the cradle of French Colonial architecture in America. After La Salle christened *La Louisiane* in honor of Louis XIV, France expanded its hold in the Mississippi Valley with the founding of the colonial capital of New Orleans in 1718. The French colony languished for decades while France and Spain sparred over territory, and its population grew slowly in the inhospitable delta. That changed when French sugar planters were forced from the island of Saint-Domingue (Haiti) by the slave rebellions of 1791 to 1803.

The expatriates headed for New Orleans with the promise of rich farmland in the French Gulf Coast

Architect Mark Finlay's new plantation house is in Spring Island, South Carolina, not Louisiana. But his French Colonial house is a modern-day example of an architectural style that has migrated from its birthplace to a new location for which it is well suited. On a waterfront site in the Carolina Low Country, the new plantation house pays homage to the homes that graced the shores of the Mississippi. Two stories tall, with a row of classical columns supporting double gallery

The two-story gallery porches and walls of French doors on this new French Colonial plantation house transplanted to the Carolina Low Country are well suited to the humid climate of the coastal plains.

Beginning in the 18th century, the banks of the Mississippi River Road were lined with sugar plantations built around gracious plantation houses with raised gallery porches facing the river.

colony. They were joined by a multicultural diaspora of French nobles escaping Napoleon's regime, Acadians (Cajuns) expelled from French Canada, Spaniards, Germans, Britons, and African *gens de couleur.* The freewheeling temperament of the Crescent City opened opportunities for all as a hub of international commerce, and, in time, it became the largest trading port in the New World.

In *Life on the Mississippi,* Mark Twain penned his admiration for the River Road from New Orleans to Baton Rouge as "a most home-like and happy-looking region." Plantation homes rose in pillared splendor along shores described by one 1827 traveler as "everywhere thickly peopled by sugar planters, whose showy houses, gay piazzas, trim gardens, and numerous slave-villages, all clean and neat, give an exceedingly thriving air to the river scenery."

During the half-century prior to the Civil War, wealthy American landowners built impressive plantations along the Mississippi, many in the Greek Revival style. Their crisp, white mansions with broad galleries and classical pillars epitomized the conspicuous lifestyle of antebellum Louisiana and are justly celebrated as the "white pillars" of the Old South. But most of the late 18th-century French Colonial plantation houses that preceded them were far less flamboyant.

Many River Road plantations were a hybrid of building solutions tested in the West Indies by Spanish, French, and English colonists before they migrated to the Gulf Coast. As they merged these traditions with influences from French Canada, Europeans of mixed ancestry created a Creole architectural style in houses well adapted to the humid, semitropical Mississippi Delta.

The main floor was raised up a full story to lift the parlors and bedrooms above the unhealthy mud flats of the bayous. Gallery porches flanked all sides to capture breezes and provide covered outdoor space for socializing, sleeping, and even bathing. Columns made

As Americans bought plantations along the Mississippi after the Louisiana Purchase of 1803, they built imposing Greek Revival mansions with two-story galleries and monumental classical pillars that were symbols of an extravagant plantation lifestyle.

The early French Colonial plantation houses were surrounded by double gallery porches to provide shade and outdoor living space. The best rooms were a full story above the bayou flats with the kitchen, workrooms, and storerooms below.

of stucco-covered brick and of turned wood rose to a French pavilion roof brought to Louisiana by Acadians from French Canada. Now known in America as the French Colonial style, this distinctive architecture was unique to the 18th-century Gulf Coast.

French Colonial in the Low Country

The Carolina Low Country and the Gulf Coast share similar climates, with summertime bouts of withering heat, high humidity, and tropical storms. Both regions also share common architectural roots in the West Indies. The architecture of the Low Country had its roots in the plantation houses of English sugar planters from Barbados. Their houses resembled those of French Creoles in the Mississippi Delta, built with the same raised foundations, open verandas, and snug rooflines.

The river front is a classic plantation house design, its long two-story galleries shaded by a pavilion roof. The gallery walls are filled with French doors that open out to river views, a signature feature of the traditional West Indies plantation style.

(opposite page) Sheltered within a copse of oaks and cypress draped with Spanish moss, the new French Colonial house is carved out of tidewater woodlands. Its three-bay-wide portico is designed with double gallery porches of classical pillars and turned wooden posts beneath a hipped roof.

Mark Finlay's choice of the French Colonial style for his new Spring Island plantation house suits both the climate and architectural traditions of South Carolina's sea island coast. Finlay's house sits on a bluff overlooking the Colleton River, a short sail from Beaufort, South Carolina.

Although not a Southern native, Finlay learned French Colonial design by studying Louisiana's plantation houses firsthand and by searching through photographs and drawings in the archives of the Historic American Buildings Survey. He has translated authentic details of French Colonial doors and transom windows, pillars and porch posts, handrails and rafter tails into a new old house.

The front entry of the house is framed by trees and clipped garden hedges that line a path to the front door. Its three-bay-wide portico is designed as a frontispiece to introduce the home's French Colonial story. The portico is a portrait in miniature of a French plantation house—a vignette of double gallery porches resting on classical pillars and turned wooden posts that rise to a hipped roof.

The best facade of the house faces the water rather than the entrance drive, an orientation that was common along the Mississippi where the river was considered the money side. The new river front is a classic plantation house, with long galleries stretched beneath a pavilion roof dotted with narrow dormer windows. Behind the gallery's columns and porch posts, walls filled with French doors open out to the river. Essentially a wall of windows, Finlay's design reproduces the historic look of French Colonial homes and, at the same time, fills the modern need for lots of light and views of a spectacular waterfront.

Adding a noble, classical character to the interiors, a hall of square Tuscan columns echoes the dignified white pillars of the gallery porch outside. Such monumental interior classicism was not part of 18th-century French Colonial plantations

French doors in all the principal rooms swing open onto gallery porches for views out to the river.

The row of French doors is a signature feature of plantation-house style, a tradition developed by European colonists in the West Indies. Designed to draw sunlight and breezes into the interior, pairs of glass doors opened up the whole house to cross ventilation. With all the doors open, air could easily circulate through interiors where few partition walls blocked the flow. Transom windows could also be cracked open for additional ventilation.

The new home's gallery porches also evoke plantation-house style, but they are unlike porches built in any other region of colonial America. Instead of two rows of classical columns stacked one on top of the other, as on Charleston's piazzas, French Colonial galleries invariably had stout Tuscan columns on the ground floor with slender turned colonnettes on the second story, just as Finlay has done at Spring Island.

Casual classical living

In a French Colonial plantation house, being able to step out of every room onto broad galleries made the best rooms even better. Naturally, the best rooms of the Spring Island house open out to the water through French doors. The living room, kitchen, and master bedroom capture the river views, while the front third of the floor plan is filled with rooms that don't need views, like the stairhall, the mudroom, pantry, laundry, and bathrooms.

Casual classical interiors begin in the stairhall, where a formal paneled staircase scissors its way from the first to second floors in a two-story foyer. A cross hall runs lengthwise through the house lined by two rows of square Tuscan columns. The columns' design reflects their counterparts on the outside gallery porches, bringing the classical details of the facade to the inside.

TELLING DETAIL

FRENCH DOORS AND TRANSOM

A classic French doorway is made of two sash-and-panel doors, where the bottom of the door is a wood panel with window panes arranged above the middle locking rail. The transom is a separate sash mounted over the doors and customarily hinged on top of the door frame to open inward.

Monumental interior classicism was not native to French Colonial architecture. There was little classical decoration inside early plantation houses, save for elegant boxed mantelpieces, molded door frames, and occasional crown moldings. Instead, the early houses were simply plastered and painted in a pastel palette of colors such as yellow ochre and moss green, beneath exposed wood ceiling beams and plank floorboards.

Plantation houses were classicized later in life when Louisiana became part of 19th-century America, and Greek Revival flourishes were added to their interiors.

Finlay's interiors reflect this higher style. The raised-panel walls, crossed ceiling beams, and refined trim moldings in the new house are painted nearly pure white for a clean, classical look that reflects sunlight throughout the interior. Because this is a modern waterside retreat meant for casual living rather than a working manor house on a sugar plantation, the liberties taken with French Colonial authenticity turn it into a real home for today instead of a museum house.

PHOTOGRAPHING THE RIVER ROAD

Appreciation for French Colonial architecture grew dramatically during the Depression, when photographer Frances Benjamin Johnston was commissioned by Andrew Carnegie to document the early American architecture of the South for study by future generations. This photographic record is now housed in the Library of Congress as the Pictorial Archives of Early American Architecture.

Johnston was the first American woman to achieve prominence as a photographer. During the early 20th century, she toured the city streets and country roads of Virginia, North Carolina, Georgia, and Louisiana in search of what remained of the region's 17th-, 18th-, and 19th-century building traditions.

TELLING DETAIL

FRENCH COLONIAL GALLERY

French Colonial galleries were made of round molded bricks piled up into pillars and coated with stucco, then sculpted in classical Tuscan column shape. Bricks were used on the ground floor because they could stand up to the moist soils and occasional flooding of the Delta country. Second-story colonnettes were made of turned wood because they were high aboveground, though remarkably delicate considering the weight of the roof they carried.

In the two-story entry foyer, a formal stairway with walls of raised paneling zigzags up to the second floor. Its lofty proportions reflect the grand scale of the interiors.

The living room and dining room share one large space with a wall of French doors opening out to the gallery. Bathed in afternoon sunlight, the pure white classical detailing of the room is softened by muted fabrics and comfortable furniture.

Johnston's lush silver gelatin prints uncovered the wealth of Louisiana's French Colonial plantations still standing in the 1930s and '40s, before they were restored and gentrified in the late 20th century. Among the best is Parlange Plantation in Pointe Coupee Parish, Louisiana, built in the 1830s. Parlange showcases the West Indies influences in French Colonial design, one of the last built in the style and still a working sugarcane plantation on 1,500 of its original 10,000 acres.

The house is a River Road classic built to endure the heat and humidity of the subtropical climate. Plantation slaves made the bricks for the raised basement, while the second-story walls are filled with bousillage that has been whitewashed.

The interior plan is typical for large plantation houses along the Mississippi, arranged as two drawing rooms in the center with bedrooms at each end. Cypress planks are tightly fit together to make the interior partition walls, floors, and ceilings. Following an old Louisiana custom, the cypress floors were originally limewashed and later scrubbed and reddened with brick dust. In 1936, New Orleans architect Richard Koch measured the construction details of Parlange, making exquisite drawings and photographs for the Historic American Buildings Survey.

NEW ORLEANS REVIVALISTS

Architects Koch and Samuel Wilson, Jr., were devoted preservationists of Louisiana's architectural heritage and New Orleans's French colonial history. They became architectural partners in 1955, and their credits include restoring the James Pitot House (see pp. 112-113), the Cabildo, Shadows-on-Teche, and Oak Alley. Wilson's pioneering survey of New Orleans's Lower Garden District was the first volume in the eight-part *New Orleans Architecture* series.

Parlange Plantation (1830s) is a classic French Colonial plantation house in Pointe Coupee Parish, Louisiana, built in response to the heat and humidity of the Mississippi Delta. Its two-story gallery porches supported by Tuscan columns with turned cypress colonnettes on the second floor provided genteel living space during the long, sultry Louisiana summers.

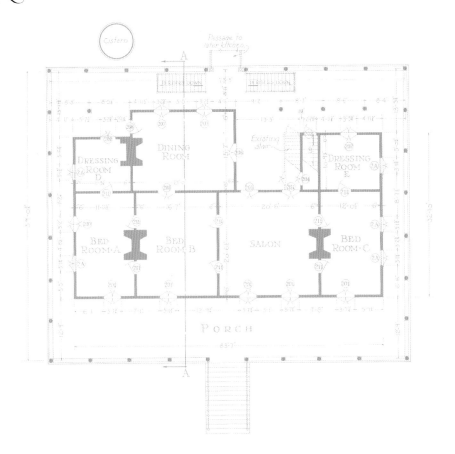

As at Parlange Plantation, the rhythmic gallery porches of French Colonial plantation houses made their exteriors look symmetrical, but the interior plans were often asymmetrical and always lacked hallways. Openings for French doors were placed more or less for convenience, creating an irregular spacing. Across the front of the house, parlors and bedrooms were linked together in a row, while rooms in the rear included an open loggia with a small room at each end called a cabinet.

Koch's design for the Donald Markel House of 1936 in Pass Christian, Mississippi, shows his appreciation for the building traditions of Creole Louisiana and his fondness for the Spanish Customs House, which he was measuring and recording at the time. In 1927, he described the old French Colonial plantation house as "the ideal house to build in this climate, for the porch in our long summers breaks the heat and gives us a home that is delightful to live in."

In the 21st century, the French Colonial plantation house has become one of the darlings of new traditional architects. Architect Ron Domin of New Orleans has re-created the James Pitot House on a street in Rosemary Beach, Florida, reproducing the historic house stick-by-stick from measured drawings prepared by New Orleans historian Eugene Cizek in 1964. Domin's generally faithful replica looks right at home at the beach amid other authentically detailed new old houses, reinventing the spirit of Gulf Coast architecture in a New Urbanist setting.

(above top) Designed by architect Richard Koch in 1936 for Donald Markel of Pass Christian, Mississippi, this re-creation of a traditional French Colonial plantation illustrates the adaptability of this classic style for modern living.

(above bottom) Using historian Eugene Cizek's measured drawings of the James Pitot House, architect Ron Domin has faithfully reprised the historic house in the New Urbanist community of Rosemary Beach, Florida.

(left) Beneath the gallery porch of Mark Finlay's new old house, French doors open from the living room to views of the river through a colonnade of Tuscan columns.

JAMES PITOT HOUSE

The house of the first mayor of New Orleans, Frenchman James Pitot, is a two-story Creole plantation house constructed in 1799 along the banks of Bayou St. John. Because the bayou was prone to flooding, the ground floor is made of brick coated with plaster, while the upper story is a heavy timber frame with brick infill of briquette-entre-poteaux. Gallery porches surround two sides of the house, their slender colonnettes supporting a hipped pavilion roof covered in cypress shingles.

The Pitots were well-to-do citizens, and their house reflects the lavish lifestyle of cosmopolitan 19th-century New Orleans. While the ground-floor rooms are built simply to temper the damage from flooding, the second floor is opulently decorated and furnished. The parlor, or *salon,* is the main living space, with bedrooms opening to either side. A carved mantelpiece with an overmantel that reaches the ceiling beams is the architectural *pièce de résistance.* French doors open up the two long sides of the room to the front and rear gallery porches.

In the French Colonial tradition, there are no hallways or stairs inside the house, so the staircase is outside in one corner of the rear loggia. One interior room opens into the next in an arrangement designed to promote cross ventilation. The ceilings are built tall to trap warm air, and doors are positioned across from one another to help breezes move through the house.

The Pitots probably spent as much time outside their home as inside. Their spacious second-floor balcony was used for entertaining and dining *en plein air.* In warm weather, beds could be pushed outside to make the gallery a large sleeping porch.

The Pitot House represents a stylish plantation house built in New Orleans just before the Louisiana Purchase. Used time and again as a model, this masterpiece is a precious resource for studying French Colonial architecture, painstakingly restored and maintained by the Louisiana Landmarks Society.

(far left) Sitting behind a traditional pieux debout *fence of split cypress stakes, the gallery porches of the Pitot House look out over Bayou St. John, an early waterway into New Orleans. The distinctive break in the roofline was revealed at the time of the restoration.*

(left) *Stairways were not considered part of the inside of the house. Instead, the staircase was often built outside, tucked into a corner of the rear* loggia *or cut into the double gallery porch.*

(below) *Featuring a sumptuous French Colonial mantelpiece with an overmantel of classical pilasters, the parlor is the principal room on the second floor. Its palette of apricot walls and sage-gray trim reveals the preference for vibrant colors in 19th-century New Orleans.*

3

OUR ENGLISH HERITAGE

CAVALIERS, PURITANS, AND BEGGARS

"Having undertaken, for the glory of God, and advancement of the Christian faith, and honor of our king and country, a voyage to plant the first colony in the northern parts of Virginia, do by these presents solemnly and mutually . . . covenant and combine ourselves together into a civil body politic, for our better ordering and preservation."

—MAYFLOWER COMPACT, November 11, 1620

Unlike the Spanish and the French, the English came to North America to stay. They focused on founding permanent settlements rather than staking claims to territory or exploiting the native people. Up and down the Atlantic Coast, the English Crown handed out land grants to populate its new colonies and to rid England of as many troublemakers and malcontents as possible.

Land grants accomplished many things for the king. They got rid of religious dissidents such as the Puritans and Quakers. They created new estates for the sons of English gentry such as John Washington, George's great-grandfather. They paid off royal debts to Cavaliers such as George Calvert, Lord Baltimore. And they were a good and relatively inexpensive way to relocate convicts, the chronically indigent, slackers, and other misfits.

From this motley mix of Englishmen came the seedbeds of American building traditions, as they adapted old-world customs to the new continent from Massachusetts Bay to the Delaware Valley, Chesapeake Bay, and the Carolina Low Country.

Importing the building traditions they knew from their homeland, the English transplanted timber-frame construction to the Atlantic seaboard. With oaks plentiful in the virgin forests, they found a familiar material to hew into homes.

(opposite page) The English settlers' first homes were primitive cottages of hewn oak timbers sided with split weatherboards and coated with tar oil to preserve and protect the wood from the weather.

BRISK BEGINNINGS IN THE NEW WORLD

Although Sir Walter Raleigh established an English colony in 1584 on Roanoke Island off North Carolina, it vanished without a trace within a few years. It was Captain John Smith who founded the first permanent colony, Jamestown, in 1607, followed in 1620 by William Bradford and the Pilgrims at Plimoth Plantation in Massachusetts. Cecil Calvert began the Maryland colony as a refuge for English Catholics in 1634, and, later in the century, Lord Anthony Ashley-Cooper and friends founded Charleston in 1670.

Within a century of the Jamestown landing, English settlements were strung together in 13 Atlantic colonies. Trading ports bustled along the New England coast. Philadelphia was a thriving center of business and culture. Prosperous plantations were taking root around the Chesapeake Bay and Carolina Low Country. By the time of the American Revolution, roughly 275,000 Europeans lived in what later became the United States. All but a handful were English.

The English brought with them what they knew about building and, as best they could, transplanted that knowledge to America. At first they built primitive imitations of the manor houses and humble cottages of the mother country; they also adapted a half-century of colonial building experiences in the West Indies to North America. Over time the houses became distinctly American in flavor, influenced by the demands of new climates, geography, and local building materials.

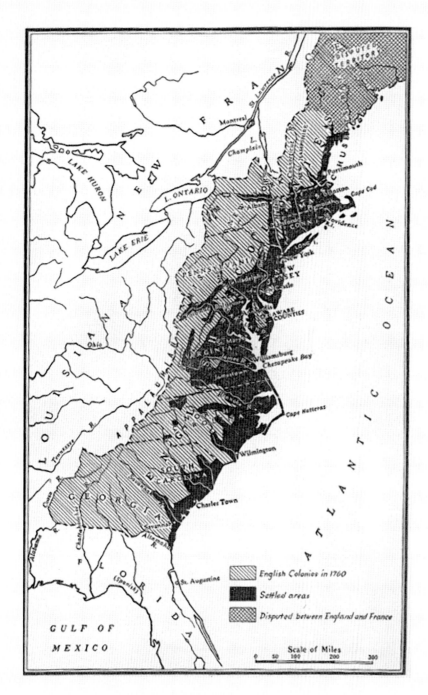

Harsh Winters, Humble Cottages

Two distinct cultures separated the English colonies of the North and the South. New England was an egalitarian experiment in community building run by stern Puritan leaders and governed by strict rules of faith, with a strong middle class of farmers, artisans, and merchants. Life was defined by the seasonal rhythms of agriculture and knit by the bonds of family, church, and community.

The colony was settled in an orderly fashion, with land parceled out evenly among families. Settlement proceeded in a tight-knit pattern of towns and cities led by Boston, the social and economic heart of New England. Houses were clustered around town commons, where the church, tavern, and fortified garrison addressed the spiritual and social needs of the settlers and provided refuge from Indian attacks.

The early houses of Massachusetts Bay mimicked the wood-frame cottages of England's Midlands and East Anglia, where the Pilgrims came from. With sturdy oak timbers plentiful, New Englanders built half-timbered houses covered with shingles and clapboards, like the tile-hung and weatherboard farmhouses of the Old Country. Their houses were solidly built to withstand the weather but scantily furnished, with little regard for comfort. From these early one-room cottages, the distinctive New England styles of the saltbox and Cape Cod cottage emerged.

Life on the Plantation

The South, by contrast, developed a plantation system in which a landed aristocracy ruled over the poor, the indentured, and the enslaved. With few exceptions, there was little or no town life, and the insignificant villages were scattered at great distances. The Tidewater coast became an agrarian countryside of self-contained plantation estates modeled on English manors and divided into Anglican parishes outside widely separated market centers such as Williamsburg and Charleston. The planters' isolation forged an acute need for social interaction and hospitality at home.

For the plantation gentry, the architecture of the South was aristocratic, while for the poor, houses were rude shacks, with little in between. The plantation houses of Maryland and Virginia were patterned after the brick manor houses of England's East Anglia, The Downs, and Thames Valley. Around Chesapeake Bay, brick making began early, and planters laid up a brick

Georgian manor as soon as tobacco profits would allow. In the Carolina Low Country, English colonists from the West Indies brought templates that became the townhouses of Charleston and the plantation houses of the Tidewater. For nearly a half-century, they had practiced building in the subtropical climate of the Caribbean; now they imported the raised plantation with its covered verandas and shallow roofs to the humid and semitropical Carolinas.

The lion's share of what became America's classic home styles can be traced to these English roots. From the English we have inherited the refined Georgian houses of New England, the Palladian brick manor houses of Virginia, the Cape Cod cottage, and the Williamsburg colonial. In the Deep South, the iconic Tidewater plantation and its gracious porches are unimaginable without the English building experience in the Caribbean. These styles have left a deep imprint on building traditions in town and country houses across America for three centuries.

Shingled cottages in the Pilgrim colony of Massachusetts Bay mimicked the farmsteads of England's Midlands and East Anglia, where late medieval houses were timber frames covered in weatherboards or hung-tile shingles beneath a thatched roof.

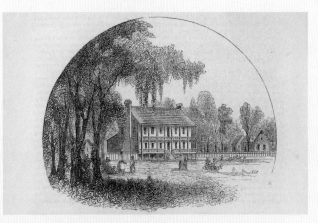

In the humid coastal marshes of the Carolina Low Country, English planters from the West Indies imported the raised plantation house surrounded by open verandas beneath shallow overhanging roofs to provide shelter and draw breezes in the sultry climate.

MARYLAND MANOR HOUSES

"Heaven and earth never agreed better to frame a place for man's habitation . . . here are mountaines, hills, plaines, valleyes, rivers and brookes, all running most pleasantly into a faire Bay compassed but for the mouth with fruitfull and delightsome land."

—CAPTAIN JOHN SMITH, *A Map of Virginia and the Proceedings of the English Colonie in Virginia* (1612)

Captain John Smith's glowing report of Chesapeake Bay's "delightsome land" reached London soon after he established the Virginia colony in 1607. Enthralled by his account of this promised land, Cecilius Calvert, Lord Baltimore, decided to colonize his New World fiefdom on the bay as a refuge for persecuted English Catholics. In 1634, Calvert sent his brothers, Leonard and George, to found St. Mary's City as the colonial capital of Maryland, the third English colony in North America.

Two historic houses overlooking St. Mary's River sit on the site of the first land grant made by Lord Baltimore. Restored to life and enlarged by architect Stephen Muse, the sister houses of West St. Mary's Manor and Porto Bello are treasured new old houses, 18th-century landmarks turned into 21st-century family homes. The Muse additions are designed in Maryland's early vernacular building traditions to blend seamlessly with the original manor houses.

HOMES OF THE CAVALIERS

Captain John Smith's Chesapeake journal of 1612 embellished the wonders of this "faire Bay" in his zeal to attract settlers to the Virginia Colony at Jamestown. His gilded prose bore fruit, and by the mid 17th century, colonies were flourishing in Virginia and Maryland, making the tidewater shores of the bay the cradle of English civilization in the New World.

In Cecilius Calvert's Maryland colony, land was divided among Lords Proprietors into large plantations, transplanting the seeds of England's manorial system to American soil. The Proprietors were English Cavaliers—loyal supporters of King Charles I—who soon discovered that tobacco thrived in the rich earth of the Maryland peninsula. Tobacco was enormously profitable in trade with England and the other American colonies, but the "vile sotweed" depleted the soil quickly, making it necessary to own thousands of acres with fields left fallow for decades.

Although the majority of Maryland's earliest settlers were indentured servants who tilled tobacco fields to earn their freedom, the 18th-century tobacco economy came to rely heavily on slaves. Fueled by slave labor, the daily life of the colony centered on self-sufficient plantations spread across great distances, fostering small-market towns for trade rather than great cities.

Captain Henry Fleet's West St. Mary's Manor represents the late 17th-century William and Mary house style of Chesapeake Bay, an English design well known to us today from Colonial Williamsburg.

Built by William Hebb II in the 1740s, Porto Bello is a center-hall brick house with a gambrel roof that represents the beginnings of the more formal Georgian style in the Maryland colony.

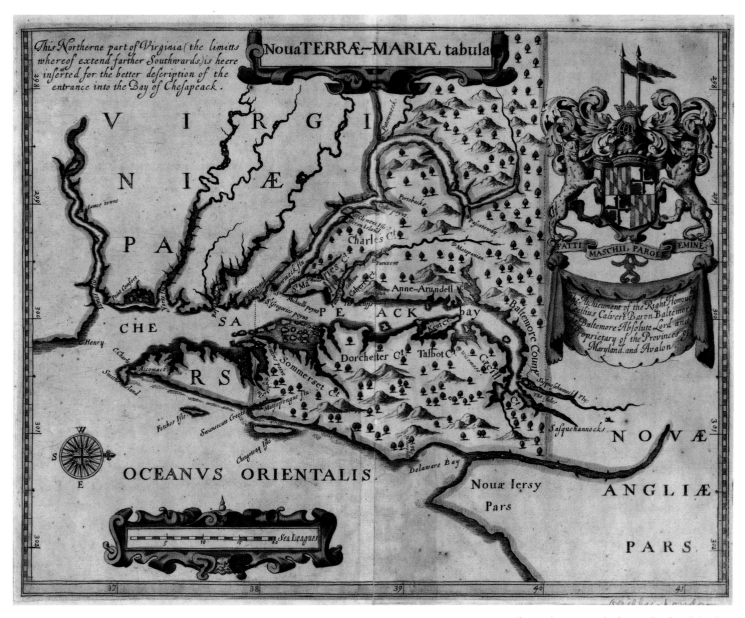

This Northerne part of Virginia (the limitts whereof extend farther Southwards) is heere inserted for the better description of the entrance into the Bay of Chesapeack.

Noua TERRÆ-MARIÆ tabula

VIRGINIÆ PARS

OCEANVS ORIENTALIS

Noua Iersy Pars

NOVÆ ANGLIÆ PARS

Chesapeake Bay was the first cradle of English colonization in America. Captain John Smith planted the Virginia Colony at Jamestown in 1607 and mapped the tidewater region for the next five years. Cecilius Calvert, Lord Baltimore, started the colony of Maryland in 1634, founding St. Mary's City as its colonial capital.

As in England, the manor house was the seat of the Lord of the Manor who had feudal powers over his land, tenants, and slaves. Maryland's planters strove to replicate the lifestyles of their English peers, but their first houses were hardly comparable, being simple timberframe cottages rather than elegant manor houses. Brick making was one of Maryland's first industries, and by the 1670s, Maryland's gentry were building more sophisticated brick houses in the Georgian style, creating some of the finest architectural treasures of early America.

GODIAH SPRAY PLANTATION

Historic St. Mary's City has re-created an early Maryland house and tobacco farm at Godiah Spray Plantation, surrounded by a kitchen garden, tobacco barns, an apple orchard, and fields of tobacco. Although constructed in 1984 for St. Mary's 250th anniversary, the timberframe house replicates the steep roof, weatherboard siding, and small diamond-pane windows of late medieval English yeoman's cottages.

Oaks were abundant in Maryland's virgin forests, and as the land was cleared the trees were cut into timber posts and beams, roof shingles, and long, thin boards for siding. On the Godiah Spray House, hand-split oak weatherboards are overlapped in rows and nailed in place over the timber frame. The walls are painted with a coat of tar oil to repel wind, rain, and rot.

With little brick making in early 17th-century Maryland, fireplaces were made of fieldstones instead, shaped into large cooking hearths that also provided heat. Chimneys were simple channels carrying smoke out the roof, built of wooden slats woven together into a tall box sealed with clay (called a Welsh chimney). Above the roof, the chimney box was covered with weatherboards.

Glass had to be imported from England in colonial times, so the windows at Godiah Spray are small. Precious glass panes were assembled in diamond-pane casements rather than double-hung sash, with glass held in place by lead channels called "cames." Because they were expensive, windows were few in number, and they were often sealed tight from the outside with plank shutters.

(left) The interiors of Godiah Spray Plantation are distinctly medieval-English in character: an early 17th-century house framed with heavy timber girder beams and rough-hewn floor joists anchored around a stone cooking hearth.

(below top) Godiah Spray is a timberframe replica of an early Maryland farmhouse. Surrounded by a kitchen garden and tobacco barns, its steep roof, weatherboard siding, and small diamond-pane windows are similar to a late medieval English yeoman's cottage.

(below bottom) Weatherboards were hand split, or "riven," from oak logs using a froe and mallet, basically a hammer and wedge driven down through the log to split off a thin plank.

The clapboard facade of surrounds the front door and transom window, which are plain and simple versions of England's 17th-century William and Mary style.

SISTER HOUSES ON THE RIVER

Restored by Stephen Muse, the sister houses on St. Mary's River represent two architectural styles that were common in the Chesapeake tidewater. West St. Mary's Manor is a story-and-a-half clapboard house with a simple gable roof and brick end walls. Porto Bello is made entirely of brick and has a double-sloped gambrel roof with a row of shed dormers.

A William and Mary manor

West St. Mary's Manor stands on a promontory high above the shore, looking across the river at the restored town of St. Mary's City. Built on land first granted to Captain Henry Fleet by Lord Baltimore in 1634, the clapboard manor house is made of heavy wooden timbers sandwiched between sturdy brick ends with double chimneys. The William and Mary-style house dates from 1700 to 1730, a period when the simple one- and two-room cottages of 17th-century Chesapeake Bay transitioned to larger and more symmetrical center-hall manor houses in the 18th century.

West St. Mary's timberframe corner posts, roof beams, wall studs, and diagonal braces are all pegged together into a wooden skeleton, a system practiced by English builders since medieval times. Spaces between posts are filled in with soft bricks, called *brick nogging*, to stabilize and insulate the outside walls. The brick end walls incorporate pairs of chimneys that reinforce the whole structure like the buttresses of a Gothic cathedral.

The original clapboard facade is spare and simple, composed of a plain front door and transom flanked by windows with paneled shutters. A prim wooden staircase leads up to a front door similar in design to those on the houses of Colonial Williamsburg. The similarity is not surprising given that the settlers of early Maryland and Virginia shared a common bond of English building traditions.

West St. Mary's Manor before restoration.

Built in the opening years of the 18th century, West St. Mary's Manor is a simple story-and-a-half timberframe house with clapboard walls and brick ends buttressed by double chimneys with a pent built between them. The timbers were infilled with soft bricks, called brick nogging, *to stabilize and insulate the walls.*

PENT CHIMNEY

West St. Mary's Manor is called a *pent chimney* house, one of several distinctive types in colonial Maryland. In this design, two chimneys were built close together with a penthouse book-ended between them. The penthouse, or *pent*, also made of brick, was a small interior closet provided with a window for daylight. The *pent* and its companion chimneys often formed the entire gable end of the house.

Clustered around the manor

The historic house is the anchor for Muse's additions, which include a living room, kitchen, sunroom, and master bedroom suite. The added space is parceled out in a connected group of buildings resembling those that clustered around an 18th-century plantation. Intentionally designed to be secondary to the original house, the additions re-create the familiar shapes of Maryland's vernacular architecture.

The front entry of West St. Mary's Manor is reminiscent of the design of homes in Colonial Williamsburg.

The most prominent addition resembles an early Maryland clapboard settler's house. Attached perpendicular to the main house, it is home to the new family room and kitchen under a cathedral ceiling of wood beams. Narrow dormer windows draw daylight into the house and, although they seem impossibly slender, are historically accurate reproductions of those on the historic house.

The unusual double-pitched roof is called a catslide, a roof that kicks out at a shallower pitch and continues the roofline over a porch. Muse fabricated a story that the old porch had been enclosed with tall sash windows in the early 20th century to create a sunroom. In summer, the windows are replaced with screens to make the room an open porch again.

Muse designed the new master bedroom wing as two connected pavilions, like the small, square storehouses and dairies built around an early Maryland manor. Built with pyramid roofs covered in shingles,

the brick pavilions are limewashed, a technique used in colonial times to protect the brickwork and mortar. Muse took pains to re-create the time-weathered finish that lets some of the brick color show through, giving the pavilions a realistic patina of age.

Preserving the pedigree

On the next point down St. Mary's River sits Porto Bello, an 18th-century brick manor, built in the 1740s by William Hebb II, that was seriously dilapidated when Muse began his work. The roof had given way, the brick walls were crumbling, and the woodwork had begun to rot. The house was practically a ruin, but the interiors were a treasure of early Georgian millwork begging to be restored. Rising to the challenge, the new owners took on the house as saviors of its past, while adding new parts to extend its life for modern living.

The catslide roof addition for the new family room and sunroom re-creates the shape of an early Maryland settler's cottage, with narrow dormer windows added to bring sunlight into the interior.

Porto Bello's unusual roof is a gambrel often associated with Dutch Colonial architecture, but there is no likely precedent for this roof shape in the Netherlands. Instead, the gambrel roof is a clever English innovation that created much-needed headroom in the attic, and it appears often on homes in early Maryland and Virginia.

Having restored the original house, Muse set about building additions that tell a fictitious story of how the historic house changed over time. Firmly attached to each end are mirror-image additions, one for the kitchen and the other for the family room. The one-story additions are designed in Colonial Revival style, with walls of windows set between square columns that support a classical cornice, an effort to integrate them with the spare colonial character of the original house.

The architect added a long covered porch to the river front of Porto Bello. Where there had been a

Porto Bello was a near ruin before Stephen Muse undertook the challenge of rebuilding its brick walls, preserving its early Georgian interior millwork, and adding new rooms for modern living.

collapsed catslide roof, there is now a new sitting porch like the one at Mount Vernon, spanning the whole length of the southern facade. A run of stout, square columns supports the porch roof, above which is a balustrade of simple spindles and square newel posts. This grand porch looks as if it was added in the 1920s, with period-appropriate classical details to match the new window wings.

Early Maryland's Georgian taste

Porto Bello is a classic center-hall Georgian house. The front door opens into a wide hallway that passes under an arch straight through the house to the river side. In colonial Maryland, the river was the highway connecting manor houses along the tidewater shore, so the best rooms—and the real front door—faced the water, not the land side.

COLONIAL MURALS

Although not antique, the hand-painted mural on the dining room walls of Porto Bello re-creates the tradition of pictorial decoration common in the colonies. In colonial times, itinerant mural painters roamed the countryside in search of commissions, painting scenes showing the life and times of the manor house. In keeping with tradition, the modern artist incorporated figures of the Lord and Lady of the Manor into this scenic view of the house and river.

The long sitting porch added onto the river front of the house is framed by a row of stout, square Tuscan columns, framing panoramic views of St. Mary's River.

The most impressive room in the house, Porto Bello's front parlor is elaborately detailed with Georgian woodwork that was saved in the restoration. Its exquisite carved mantelpiece of fluted pilasters, dentils, and scrollwork is the focal point of the room. Missing details in the plaster ceiling medallion were re-created by sculpting pieces of bubble gum.

The new sun-drenched family room is lined on three sides with floor-to-ceiling casement windows. Rough-hewn ceiling beams carry plank floorboards that span the width of the room.

room and a snug study are on the front of the house. Each room has a fireplace that appears as one of four chimneys on the outside end walls.

Carefully restored by Muse, the formal parlor is elaborately detailed with Georgian crown moldings, door casing trims, and interior shutters that fold out of paneled window jambs. The focal point is a carved mantelpiece and overmantel designed like a picture frame, beneath a round ceiling medallion of cast plaster.

Muse added two new rooms to old Porto Bello, the family room and the kitchen. Each is bright with sunlight streaming through windows that fill three walls. The ceilings are 10 ft. tall, carried by rough-hewn antique beams with wooden planks for ceiling boards.

Four rooms of unequal size fill out the original floor plan. The best rooms are the parlor and drawing room, now a library, both with tall 12-over-12 windows that face St. Mary's River. A small mural-decorated dining

The new kitchen wing addition has oversized windows set between Tuscan pilaster columns.

A jerkin-head roof is another common Chesapeake tidewater type, where the gable ends are clipped off at an angle, as on Swan Tavern (1720s) in Yorktown, Virginia. The pyramid-roof storehouses at Swan Tavern inspired Muse's master bedroom pavilions at West St. Mary's Manor.

The effect leaves you wondering whether these rooms are new or just recently updated—the perfect puzzle for a new old house.

CHESAPEAKE TIDEWATER TRADITIONS

The colonial architecture of Chesapeake Bay that inspired Muse typically lagged behind the latest styles in England by 50 years. Maryland's 17th-century manor houses were based on medieval English traditions rather than Georgian styles, with steeply pitched roofs and heavy timber framing rather than refined classical details.

A good example is the now demolished Scotch Neck, one of the oldest houses in Maryland, built in 1640 by Thomas Cornwallis, grandfather of Lord Charles Cornwallis who surrendered to George Washington. Its telltale medieval roots show in its extremely

steep roof and shallow brick arches over the windows. A similar design can be seen on the Virginia side of Chesapeake Bay, where the 1725 Rolfe House in Surry County shares the same brickwork and steep roof. Both houses were laid in Flemish bond brick—a pattern where bricks alternate between stretchers (long faces) and headers (brick ends). The brick ends were often glazed by overburning in the kiln, turning the clay into colored glass.

In colonial days, English details moved seamlessly across the bay between Virginia and Maryland. On both shores the common roof shapes were either a simple gable or a gambrel, as on West St. Mary's Manor and Porto Bello. Another variation was the roof on Swan Tavern (1720s) in Yorktown, Virginia, where the gable ends were clipped off at an angle, called a jerkinhead roof. The pyramid-roof storehouses at Swan Tavern are the tidewater model that inspired Muse's master bedroom pavilions at West St. Mary's Manor.

Maryland's 17th-century manor houses were derived from medieval English roots, a narrow two-room house, one and a half stories tall, with a steeply pitched roof. Scotch Neck (above) is a mid 17th-century example laid in Flemish bond brickwork. Rolfe House (1725) in Surry County, Virginia, is a house of similar design (left).

RISE OF PALLADIAN STYLE

For 60 years the Maryland colony prospered around its original capital of St. Mary's City, which served as the seat of the government, parish church, and trading port for a thriving plantation economy. But political forces in England pressured King William III to wrest control from the Catholic-leaning province and move the statehouse farther north toward Anne Arundel County, which was firmly committed to the Anglican faith.

The capital was moved to Annapolis in 1694, after which St. Mary's City withered and the center of settlement moved up the bay, followed by sophisticated architectural patrons. The new Palladian style imported from England soon found favor with Maryland's gentry, and country houses based on the symmetrical villas of the Italian master began to appear around Annapolis in the 1750s.

When William Paca, an Annapolis lawyer who was the Revolutionary governor of Maryland, built his Palladian townhouse in the capital in 1765, he erected a three-story brick manor with symmetrical wings. His five-part plan—a main block with two equal wings (hyphens) attached to larger pavilions (flankers)—epitomized the new style. A gifted amateur, Paca probably designed the house himself with help from English

TELLING DETAIL

STEPPED-BACK CHIMNEY

The chimney on the Revell West House is a classic Chesapeake tidewater design shared by Maryland and Virginia houses. Tapered in hipped sections from a hefty base to a slender chimney top, the bottom was wide enough to accommodate a large interior cooking hearth. The uppermost section was often offset from the wall to keep heat away, especially on wooden houses prone to catch fire.

Architect William Lawrence Bottomley revived Chesapeake Bay's 18th-century Palladian country houses in the 1920s. Many of his best houses were built in Virginia, where he designed interpretations of James River plantations such as Westover (shown here) and Colonial Revival estates such as Milburne in the Richmond suburb of Windsor Farm.

pattern books, especially Isaac Ware's translation of Palladio's *Four Books of Architecture.*

Mathias Hammond hired the most prominent carver-architect of the period, William Buckland, to design his 1777 manor. Buckland, schooled in London as a joiner, began his career in Virginia working on George Mason's Gunston Hall and John Tayloe's Mt. Airy before setting up shop in Annapolis in 1772. His Palladian design for the Hammond-Harwood House is among America's most elegant, influenced by the pattern books of James Gibbs, Abraham Swan, and Batty Langley.

FROM TIDEWATER MANOR TO SUBURBAN MCMANSION

The Chesapeake Bay's 18th-century Palladian country houses were revived in the 1920s by architects such as William Lawrence Bottomley (1883–1951). Many of Bottomley's finest works were built in Virginia, especially in the Richmond suburb of Windsor Farms, where he was a central figure in the Colonial Revival movement.

Borrowing ideas from Virginia's Anglo-Palladian past, Bottomley designed interpretations of the great James River plantations like Westover (1726) and Carter's Grove (1753) for Richmond's wealthy elite. He also designed the Colonial Revival Milburne Estate (1934), a classic five-part brick house built on a bluff overlooking the James River.

Unfortunately, the 1920s Colonial Revival took a bad turn later in the century as homebuilders threw up neo-colonial versions of American Georgian manors for the mass market. Plain brick builder boxes proliferated across the country, with poor imitations of classical porticoes applied to suburban tract homes. The trend continues today in the clumsy Georgian McMansions that are standard issue in every builder's suburban toolbox.

The William Paca House (1765) and Hammond-Harwood House (1777) are Annapolis brick manor houses inspired by the Palladian style imported to Maryland from 18th-century England. They are symmetrical villas based on the five-part plans of Italian architect Andrea Palladio, with a main block and two end pavilions attached by small hyphen wings.

CONNECTICUT RIVER VALLEY COLONIAL

"The early Connecticut house…was a new creation, wherein the use of materials and the manner of construction were largely the result of Old World tradition, modified to meet an entirely new and different set of conditions."

—J. FREDERICK KELLY, *The Early Domestic Architecture of Connecticut* (1924)

A dozen years after landing at Plymouth, the Pilgrims had outgrown their boundaries and were looking for a place to start a new settlement. Attracted to a fertile valley on the banks of the Connecticut River, they established the village of Windsor in 1633, thereby beginning the colony of Connecticut. Three hundred fifty years later in the same town, builder Edward Sunderland began creating his own village of New England colonial homes called Settlement Hill.

As on early New England homes, the beveled clapboards on Bronson House in Settlement Hill are graduated in exposure, with boards lapped tightly together at the bottom of the wall and farther apart as they go up.

Settlement Hill is an architectural primer for the Connecticut River Valley style, from simple saltbox to garrison colonial to Georgian manor. Of the 12 homes in the new village, some are reconstructions of historic houses, while others are authentic reproductions. Sunderland's trademark homes are so convincing that it is nearly impossible to tell which is old and which is new. It really doesn't matter because these new old houses are not museum houses: They are meant for real people to live in.

NEW ENGLAND VILLAGES

By the 1630s, the Pilgrims and their Puritan cousins had successfully established a beachhead on the New England coast in towns that bore the nostalgic names of their homeland—Plymouth, Boston, and Dorchester, among others. They were soon overwhelmed by new arrivals and needed room to grow, which they did not by enlarging their compact villages but by starting new settlements elsewhere, with their own meetinghouses, common greens, and village elders. Thus began the New England pattern of many small but interrelated towns spread across the landscape.

When the colonists of Plimoth Plantation were secure enough to build permanent homes, they constructed post-and-beam houses with steep roofs covered in thatch. The spaces between posts were infilled with clay-and-straw cob and sheathed with riven clapboards.

Connecticut was the western frontier for the colonists of Massachusetts Bay. In the 1630s, three separate groups of pioneers found their way to the Connecticut River, founding the towns of Windsor, Wethersfield, and Hartford each within a day's walk. Each town depended upon the others for protection against the Pequot Indians. Windsor's perimeter was fortified with a *palizado,* or palisade, of vertical logs set into the ground, within which stood a meetinghouse, a parsonage, and a half-dozen homes built around a common green.

From cottage to saltbox

Windsor's first meetinghouse arrived along with the Pilgrims in their boat from Plymouth, its knocked-down timber frame and siding ready to be "clapt up." William Bradford tells the tale in his 1647 journal, *Of Plimoth Plantation:*

"Having made a smale frame of a house ready, and haveing a greate new barke, they stowed their frame in her hold, & bords to cover & finishe it . . . Coming to their place, they clapt up their house quickly, and landed their provisions . . . and afterwards palisadoed their house aboute."

More houses followed as the settlers cleared fields of oaks and squared them with broadaxes into posts and beams. These post-and-beam houses were pegged together, with the spaces between timbers filled with a mixture of unbaked clay and straw called cob (similar to French bousillage). Riven clapboards covered the walls, the steep roof was thatched with straw, and a

By the 1630s, the Pilgrims and Puritans had established colonies on the New England coast at Plymouth and Boston. Overwhelmed by new arrivals, they searched for locations for new settlements, founding the Connecticut colony in 1633.

The steep roofs and one-room floor plans of the houses of Plymouth were adaptations of the yeomen's farmhouses of England. The Pilgrims were familiar with this traditional type and built simple versions using materials close at hand in the new colony.

The Evolution of
the New England House Plan

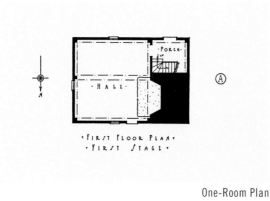

One-Room Plan

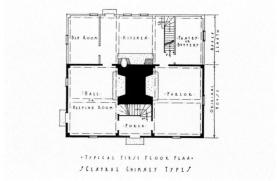

Lean-To Plan

Hall-and-Parlor Plan

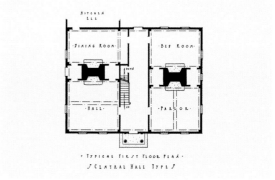

Center-Hall Plan

The New England colonial house developed through several stages, beginning as a single room with a fireplace. Adding a second room opposite the fireplace created a hall-and-parlor plan, onto which a saltbox lean-to was often added across the back. Only after about 1750 did the classic center-hall New England colonial come into vogue.

chimney of woven sticks covered in mud stood on the gable end.

These homes resembled the one-room cottages built by yeoman farmers in England's Midlands and East Anglia, the Pilgrims' former homeland. But a cottage was suitable only for the smallest of families, and many enlarged their homes by adding onto the chimney end, making the fireplace the center of the house. As the family grew, still more space was needed. By adding a lean-to across the back, they created a house shaped like

a traditional English saltbox, and a New England classic was born. The two front rooms became the hall and parlor in the saltbox design, while the lean-to housed the keeping room kitchen and two smaller rooms—a borning room and a buttery.

The center-hall house that we think of today as the archetypal New England colonial did not appear until about 1750 when the new Georgian style arrived from England, with a floor plan that had become fashionable in London 30 years earlier. Now a center hall ran through the middle of the house with two rooms laid out symmetrically on each side. From then on, the four-room center-hall colonial became a common fixture throughout New England.

A Connecticut Yankee Craftsman

Edward Sunderland is a New England antiquarian—a Yankee builder and craftsman with a passion for history and a zeal for creating authentic new old houses. His 10-year odyssey at Settlement Hill fulfilled his dream of building a village of homes patterned after the regional traditions of the Connecticut River Valley. Although his new village is not built around a common green, the dozen houses there represent a walking tour through Connecticut's colonial past.

The paneled fireplace wall of the Bronson House is typical of the building traditions of the Connecticut River Valley.

(left) Adding a lean-to across the back of a house created the classic New England saltbox design. The reconstructed Jonathan Bronson House (1680s) is a timberframe house that was dismantled and moved to Settlement Hill from Brookfield, Connecticut, where it had suffered from years of benign neglect.

Two longtime village residents live in the Jonathan Bronson House, a 1987 reconstruction built around the timber frame of a 1680s saltbox from Brookfield, Connecticut. The early structure was dismantled and moved to Settlement Hill to become the second house in the village. In his reconstruction, Sunderland built a new kitchen and pantry in the 1740s saltbox addition and added a rear ell as a bedroom wing.

Early New England saltboxes like Bronson House were plain and simple affairs, tokens of Puritan pragmatism and frugality. Ornament was discouraged except for the front door, which was the decorative threshold of the house. Doorways were a distinctive art form in the Connecticut River Valley, and Sunderland has re-created many of them at Settlement Hill. There are doorways with transom windows, classical pilasters, and elaborately scrolled pediments each representing one of the classic styles.

TELLING DETAIL

YANKEE V-GUTTER

The gutters on Bronson House are two boards joined together in a V-shape and hung from the box cornice on wooden brackets—a common New England detail. They channel rainwater into round downspouts that run down the wall inside wooden boxes. Colonists used gutters and downspouts to prevent rot by keeping rainwater from splashing up onto siding boards.

As Sunderland rebuilt the house, he converted the 1740s saltbox addition into a kitchen and dining room, while adding a new rear ell for an extra bedroom and bath.

(opposite page) Bronson House reveals the plain-and-simple austerity of New England's early colonists, who built homes for practical shelter rather than decorative display. Except for the decorative portico around the front door, the details are relentlessly spare.

CONNECTICUT VALLEY DOORWAYS

Doorways were a distinctive art form in the Connecticut River Valley, which Edward Sunderland has re-created in many forms at Settlement Hill. The doorway was the most elaborate decorative feature on the house, designed as a classical portico of columns supporting a pediment that framed the front door. Often built using English pattern books as guides, pediments went from plain to fancy, shaped as simple cornices, triangles, arches, and complex scrolls of curved woodwork.

Sunderland has crafted the most ordinary details with historical accuracy. The front door surround is a plain triangular pediment, while the window frames are square boards with no decorative trim. Although many Georgian Colonial houses had elaborate moulded cornices, here the cornice is a simple box with no crown mouldings and the corner boards are flat instead of classical pilasters.

For historical accuracy, the new double-hung windows are pegged together and single-glazed with old cylinder glass. Since there are no counterweights to hold them open, each window comes with a notched stick to prop it up for ventilation.

(right) The small entry foyer of a classic New England saltbox was called a "porch", used to keep cold air out of the house when the door was opened. A staircase to the second floor was pressed tight against the massive chimney at the center of the house.

A compact saltbox plan

The front door of Bronson House opens into a classic saltbox entryway, called a porch in colonial times. This tiny porch served as a vestibule to buffer the inside of the house from blasts of cold air. A tight winder stair sits against the back wall, built only as wide as the chimney that anchors the center of the house. The stair is compact and steep because it was meant to be practical rather than gracious.

The interior floor plan is a late saltbox type that predates the classic center-hall plan. In Sunderland's updated version, the two front rooms are the hall and parlor, with the kitchen and dining room where the traditional keeping room would have been. In the old house, the hall was the kitchen, confirmed by its enormous cooking hearth and built-in bake oven reconstructed with replica handmade bricks. A stout oak manteltree beam spans the fireplace to support the stone chimney.

Lest we think that the house walls are made of lightweight studs, Sunderland has left exposed the corner posts and beams of the original timber frame. Heavy oak floor joists span the ceilings to support plank floorboards above, locked into massive beams called girts that run from front to back of the house.

Colonial builders used oak for timber framing, even though it was hard to cut and shape, because it was unsurpassed for strength. Oak framing was a tradition handed down from the Old Country, where generations of English woodwrights counted on its durability. For New Englanders, permanence was an obsession, and the many timberframe colonial homes still standing are testimony to their skill in building.

In the 1740s lean-to addition, where the original keeping room had been, is a new dining room with a wall of reproduction raised paneling. Beyond is the back stair to the new rear ell for the bedroom addition.

Sunderland restored the fireplace and original paneled wall of the cooking hearth in the old hall of Bronson House. The massive manteltree beam over the fireplace was salvaged from the historic structure.

A Window on New England's Past

A trove of colonial saltboxes similar to the Bronson House survive to this day across New England, many dating to the late 1600s. Among the earliest and most medieval in character, the Jethro Coffin House in Nantucket is known as the "Oldest House." Built in 1686 by the grandson of Tristram Coffin, one of the earliest settlers, this original saltbox has a steep roof, small diamond-pane windows, and a stout central chimney. Inside, the post-and-beam frame has gunstock corner posts shaped like their namesake to support massive beams that carry the floor joists.

Also of early date, the John Bradford House near Plymouth, Massachusetts, is a classic saltbox that reveals traces of its growth over time. The original house of 1674 included the central chimney and only one room, later extended to the north with a parlor

Jethro Coffin built his Nantucket house in 1686, the oldest house on the island. It is distinctly medieval in character, with a steep roof and diamond-pane windows.

Homes of Settlement Hill

The Bronson saltbox is not the only authentic home at Settlement Hill. The Benjamin Moore House of 1770 (above left) is a stately garrison colonial that Edward Sunderland relocated from its original Windsor, Connecticut, site, adding a rear kitchen ell and attached garage.

The garrison style is distinctive because its second-floor walls extend beyond the first floor by almost a foot, especially on the front facade. The design is erroneously attributed to frontier forts, called garrisons, where the overhangs were used to repel Indian attacks, but the garrison design was a familiar form in medieval England.

The Glebe House (above right) is a brand-new reproduction of a 1750 historic original in Woodbury, Connecticut. This gambrel-roof colonial is so called because its roof has a double pitch to provide extra headroom in the attic, with a saltbox extension on the back side. The house is painted melon rose with dark forest green trim that, though not an authentic colonial palette, is certainly eye-catching.

ROYAL BARRY WILLS HOUSE

⌇⌇⌇⌇⌇

Royal Barry Wills's own house built on an old estate just outside of Boston shows the range of liberties he took with the Cape style while still retaining its authentic character. His house hugs low to the ground with eaves just above the windows and an oversize central chimney that anchors the house. The floor plan strays from the original's in a layout that blends the traditional four-room Cape with a L-shaped wing for the kitchen, bedrooms, and baths, and a garage configured like an old barn.

and lean-to addition across the back. A few of its diamond-pane casement windows survive, while others are double-hung sash that probably replaced earlier casements. Its wall shingles have weathered to gray, each one 3 ft. long to overlap twice and fastened in place with forged iron nails.

HUMBLE REVIVAL

The beauty of the colonial houses of New England went unnoticed for nearly 200 years until it was rediscovered in the 1890s by young architects such as Charles Follen McKim (1847–1909) and Arthur Peabody (1858–1942). In a burst of colonial enthusiasm rekindled by the Philadelphia Centennial of 1876, architects began to search for the roots of distinctly American architectural styles as inspiration for designing modern homes.

The Colonial Revival that followed reinvented the New England Georgian in classical variations suited to contemporary lifestyles. Throughout the building boom of the 1920s, the simple saltbox and its humble relative, the Cape Cod cottage, were overlooked by architects as being too primitive to be taken seriously.

That all changed with the Great Depression. In the new reality, the uncomplicated simplicity of the saltbox and the Cape offered workable plans for more modest, yet still authentic, versions of home. By the 1930s, designs for Capes began to appear regularly in popular

magazines and in home builders' catalogs such as Sears, Roebuck and Co.'s *Modern Homes*.

The undisputed master of the Cape Cod revival was architect Royal Barry Wills (1895–1962) of Boston, whose personal style was synonymous with New England traditions. Studying the early colonial houses still standing in the 1920s, Wills deftly absorbed their spare lines and intimate appeal into new homes, while adding modern features such as kitchens, family rooms, and garages.

Wills was a prolific writer on the benefits of smaller homes for people of modest means, publishing a half-dozen books of plans for small homes that were "a delight to the eye and easy on the pocketbook." Beginning with *Houses for Good Living* in 1940, he authored *Better Houses for Budgeteers* the following year, both with plans for those who "have to budget before they build." To the little guy looking for an affordable home, Wills became a folk hero.

The John Bradford House (1674) grew by stages from a single-room house to a hall-and-parlor home with a later lean-to addition.

Long handsplit shingles and diamond-pane casement windows were common on early New England colonials.

SAMUEL MULFORD HOUSE

uilt in 1680 in the village of East Hampton, New York, Mulford Farm and its 14 acres was home to the Mulford family until 1949. At the time the timberframe house was built, East Hampton was a well-established English colonial village on Long Island, settled by colonists from Massachusetts Bay who had brought their traditional ways of life and building techniques with them.

The house survives with most of its original construction unchanged since 1750, when David and Rachel Mulford built a lean-to addition across the back to create a saltbox. Their addition was a typical solution to spatial problems faced by many colonists, as well as a reflection of changing tastes in mid 18th-century New England. The Mulfords' lean-to not only solved the need for a bigger kitchen but also made a fashionable home remodeling statement.

Next door to Mulford Farm, the John Howard Payne House of 1720 was built from the ground up in the saltbox style (now a museum for the composer of "Home Sweet Home"). Its restored windmill is a tribute to Dutch influences in the building history of Long Island, where, in the early 17th century, coastal winds were harnessed to power everything from sawmills to grinding wheels.

A New England saltbox built in East Hampton, New York, Mulford Farm (1680) has been restored to its 1750s appearance.

The windmill of the John Howard Payne House (1720), next door to Mulford Farm, was a typical feature used as a source of power on Long Island homesteads.

(below) The classic saltbox design resulted from adding a lean-to across the back of the original hall-and-parlor house. Such additions were common in New England when additional space was need for a keeping room kitchen, the place where the family did most of the household chores.

ANGLO-CARIBBEAN PLANTATION

"In the matter of design the Low Country seems to have followed those current in England, with a differencing caught from the West Indies....The straightforward piazza as used in Barbadoes...was only too often allowed to swarm over Low Country houses with the exuberant inclusiveness of wild figs strangling jungle trees."
—SAMUEL GAILLARD STONEY, *Plantations of the Carolina Low Country* (1938)

Along the back roads of the South, old houses stand neglected in fields that once hummed with the planting and harvesting of rice, cotton, and sugarcane. Their stories are forgotten until an adventurous old-house lover comes to their rescue. On South Carolina's coastal plains west of Beaufort, one intrepid adventurer has taken the salvaged bones of old Langford House and turned it into something new.

In the 17th century, the British West Indies, especially the sugar islands of Barbados and Jamaica, fostered the plantation culture that was imported to the Carolina Low Country.

The core of the new old house is an early 20th-century raised cottage that Jim Strickland, David Bryant, and the architects at Historical Concepts have reinvented as an authentic Low Country tidewater plantation. In its heyday, Langford was a simple wood-frame farmhouse with a porch across the front, raised above the moist, sandy coastal soils on concrete piers. Haphazard additions accumulated over time clung to its walls, disguising its simple, graceful lines. Historical Concepts stripped old Langford of its tattered add-ons, picked it up off its piers, and moved it to a new site to be reborn.

Set within a piney woodland beside a man-made pond, Langford House re-creates authentic Low Country plantation house style. Historical Concepts built it around the core of an early 20th-century farmhouse moved to the site.

The plantation houses of the Carolina Low Country were introduced by English planters from the West Indies who brought the concept of a raised house surrounded by verandas to the humid climate of the tidewater coast.

WEST INDIES IN THE CAROLINAS

The new house is in the Carolina Low Country, part of colonial America tied to England by an obscure route. In the 17th century, the islands of the British West Indies were way stations for English yeoman farmers en route to the New World. Barbados (1627) and Jamaica (1655) were the most populous English islands, prospering after the Dutch introduced the cultivation of sugarcane in 1640. But sugar was a blessing and a curse. Raising sugarcane enriched the English colonists but required large plantations and vast pools of slave labor, forcing small farmers to sell out to better-financed landowners.

By 1670, many English planters headed for the mainland in search of cheaper land, especially to the tidewater coast around Charleston. Life in the tropical islands had taught the English valuable lessons about building in a hot and humid climate. They developed plantation houses to shade them from the sun, catch cooling breezes, ward off humid air, and withstand the fury of tropical storms.

Anglo-Caribbean plantations were raised up on coral stone blocks that let air circulate underneath the floor to displace heat and humidity. Deep verandas surrounded all four sides to provide shade and to encourage the slightest breeze, while louvered shutters hung over the windows for protection. Shallow roofs sheltered the house from tropical downpours and let the fearsome winds of hurricane season roll over the top.

When the islanders packed their bags for the mainland, they brought the Anglo-Caribbean style with them. The Low Country plantation house was distinctly different from the late medieval and early Georgian houses built by colonists in Virginia and New England. Its design was right at home in the skein of tidal rivers, swamps, and savannahs along the Carolina coast, the perfect terrain for planting rice and indigo. Stands of longleaf pine and cypress thrived in the sand hills and wetlands, providing timber for building everything from heavy wooden frames to roof shingles, clapboard siding, and cabinetwork.

TELLING DETAIL

GABLE-ON-HIP ROOF

Imported from West Indies plantations, a gable-on-hip roof begins with a traditional gable roof over the core of the house, with hipped roofs stretched around it on four sides to form a skirt of shallower pitch. This skirt typically covers open piazzas, especially on French and English colonial houses in the Gulf Coast and Carolina Low Country.

RENOVATING A HOUSE WITH HISTORY

Historical Concepts has reinvented Langford to look like an Anglo-Caribbean plantation and in the process provided a textbook lesson in renovating a house with history. Dating back to 1914, old Langford House was a forlorn Carolina tidewater farmhouse with strong bones to build on. The house stood on a site 20 miles away and was transported by truck to new ground, where it now sits in a clearing surrounded by hundreds of acres of pine forests.

Originally a backcountry farm, Langford House has been transformed from a humble farmhouse to an elegant Low Country plantation through authentic additions. The architects encased the core of the original house in a new shell, leaving only the shape of the old gable roof showing. The house is surrounded by a new veranda—called a piazza in the Deep South—that

stretches around the outside as a shady outdoor living room. Covering the house and its piazza is a gable-on-hip roof, a taut umbrella fanned out on four sides to shield the piazza from the sun and rain.

The porch on the old house was enclosed to provide spaces for the kitchen and master bedroom under shallow roofs. A family room with windows on three sides stretches across the back, while dormers run along the main roof to bring daylight into the upstairs bedrooms.

In colonial times, cypress and longleaf pine covered the swamps and sand hills of the coastal plains and became the primary building materials of the Carolina Low Country. Sturdy longleaf pine worked well for structural timbers and floorboards, while cypress, a naturally rot-resistant wood, was ideal for clapboards and roof shingles. Instead of cypress shingles, the roof at Langford is standing-seam metal, a material that replaced many old shingle roofs in the South in the late 19th century.

(top right) Pond Bluff (1820), a Santee River farmhouse that resembles the original Langford House before renovations, is a small raised plantation house with a simple gable roof and shallow catslide porches extended out on the front and back sides.

(left) The original back-country farmhouse is almost invisible behind new dormers and a wraparound piazza. The center section showing beneath the gable roof and chimneys is historic.

(opposite page) In the Low Country, the verandas on West Indies-style plantation houses were called piazzas. They stretched around the house as a living room sheltered from the sun and rain, used for socializing and even sleeping outdoors.

PERIOD KITCHEN

To incorporate a modern kitchen into Langford House without sacrificing authenticity, the architects made the kitchen look like an early 20th-century remodeling, as if part of the piazza had been enclosed to make the new room. The kitchen is furnished with simple cupboards and countertops and an old-fashioned farm sink. The wall cabinets are designed to look like the mail-order millwork you could buy from the Sears, Roebuck and Co. catalog in the 1920s.

Greek Revival recall

Greek Revival details were popular in the Old South from 1820 to 1865, a time when Americans drew parallels between their new democracy and the ancient Greek Republic. Recalling that history, Historical Concepts added three dormers shaped like small Greek temples onto the roof of Langford. They are classically detailed with pilaster columns at the corners that support triangular pediments to form the dormer roofs. Tall double-hung windows wrap around the front of

Known throughout the South as a tin roof, a standing-seam metal roof is made of long, thin sheets of steel that are seamed together at their edges and stand in rows that run down the roof. To keep the steel from rusting, the sheets are hot-dipped in an alloy of lead and tin—just like a tin can.

(above top) Popular in the South before the Civil War, the Greek Revival style was used as a decorative motif for detailing prominent features. At Langford House, the front entrance is a simplified Greek Revival portico of corner pilaster columns and a plain entablature beam.

(above bottom) The tall double-hung windows across the front of the house are an unusual design in which the bottom sash raises into a pocket at the top of the window frame to allow a walkout onto the piazza.

(left) In the dining room, walls and ceilings of painted beadboard with a smoky patina surround floor-to-ceiling double-hung windows that flood the interior with sunlight.

the house and are an upgrade from the simple sash on the original farmhouse. They reach from floor to ceiling in two unequal sections, where the meeting rail is high enough to walk under from inside the house onto the piazza. The piazza is an outdoor living room, a place to sit in the evening and even sleep outdoors at night.

Humble on the inside

The interiors of Langford are strikingly simple. Plain moldings trim identical doorways that mark the front and back of the original farmhouse. The main staircase is made of a square newel post and simple balusters. These unassuming details remind us that this was a working farmhouse, not an elegant plantation manor. To be practical, the walls and ceilings are painted beadboard, a traditional finish that makes sense in this humid climate because moisture and mildew won't harm the paneling and it can be scrubbed clean.

The floors are antique heart pine, some of it reused from the original house. A tradition throughout the Old South, heart pine was prized for its strength and durability and was used for structural timbers as well as for floors. Today, the old-growth forests have been harvested to extinction.

BRICK FOUNDATION PIERS

Like the houses of the British West Indies, Langford is elevated aboveground on brick foundation piers. These brick footings raise the house out of the damp soil, keeping critters away from the framing and allowing air to circulate underneath the floor to prevent rot and keep the house cool. The piers have a coarse, antique texture because the bricks are molded by hand in wooden forms lined with sand, a traditional brick-making technique.

Small design features add authentic character to the interiors of Langford. In all of the rooms, period lighting fixtures hang from the walls and ceilings. There are wall sconces, chandeliers, and even table lamps stamped with ornamental filigree. Bulbs glow behind old glass shades, adding historic luster to this new old house based on traditional precedents.

CUES FROM PLANTATIONS PAST

The key to creating an authentic new old house is to unlock the story of its precedents—where a historic style came from and why it worked well in the place it was built. Traditions are customary ways of building that are well adapted to the climate and geography of a place and, as such, the ultimate form of "green" building. It doesn't matter what region you are building in, study must always come first.

In the Carolina Low Country that radiates from Charleston in the basins of the Edisto, Ashley, Cooper, and Santee rivers, tidewater plantation culture took root in large farms of hundreds, even thousands of acres where rice, indigo, and cotton were grown. By the early 19th century, elegant plantations had risen all along the coastal plains from Savannah to Georgetown.

The plantation house was the heart of a working farm, where the proprietor lived during spring planting and fall harvesting, while his family spent the rest

The simple detailing of the staircase and trim moldings in the front entry hall is meant to convey the story that Langford was a working plantation house rather than a sophisticated country manor.

The kitchen is designed to look like it was an alteration, a new room enclosed on one corner of the piazza, *as was often done on historic plantation houses.*

of the year in the city. Inspired by West Indies models, most plantations featured a raised piazza and were often embellished with Georgian, Federal, and Greek Revival details. Many tidewater plantations were destroyed during the Civil War, leaving us a diminished legacy of restored homes to study and learn from.

William Sinkler built Eutaw Plantation in 1808 along the Santee River with a low spreading roofline and broad piazzas surrounding the story-and-a-half house. Its brick arcades supporting a raised piazza are unique for a West Indies-style house, although the slender turned cypress columns carrying the porch roof are typical. Split cypress weatherboards cover the walls up to the gable ends, and, as on Langford, three simple dormers are spaced across the roof to let sunlight into upstairs bedrooms.

A blueprint for Historical Concepts' design of Langford House, Roselawn Plantation is a classic West Indies-style plantation built on the banks of the Savannah River. Begun in 1835 by Joseph Alexander Lawton, Roselawn's piazza originally wrapped around the house on three sides, but the ends were later enclosed to create more room. As at Langford, the symmetrical floor plan has a narrow stair hall that runs through the center flanked by pairs of rooms.

Roselawn is a story and a half tall with a simple gable-on-hip roof. Its piazza is supported by square classical columns and an entablature beam that add Greek Revival touches to the design. The roof is made of standing-seam tin added over an old shingle roof in about 1900. Langford's three rooftop dormers mirror those on Roselawn, incorporating an authentic precedent into the new old house.

PLANTATION REVIVAL

After the devastation of the Civil War, the Deep South suffered a long decline through the next half century. Many elegant antebellum homes were abandoned, sold for land, or torn down, their owners unable to pay the upkeep and taxes. With the end of the Old South, the regional traditions of architecture also died out. Not

The gable-and-hip roof of Eutaw Plantation (1808), surrounded by a piazza *on three sides, is a historic precedent for the shape of Langford House, although its arched brick foundation is a unique feature.*

Practically a blueprint for Langford House, Roselawn Plantation (1835) is a raised plantation house from the Greek Revival period with a wraparound piazza *and three rooftop dormers that mirror those on Langford.*

until a measure of prosperity returned in the early 20th century did anyone bother to revive the heritage of the plantation house.

By the 1920s, Atlanta rose as the leading city of the New South and bred a school of traditional architects eager to reinvent the regional vernacular. Among them were J. Neel Reid, Philip Trammel Schutze, Lewis Edmund Crook, Jr., and James Means. These Southern revivalists rediscovered the plantation house and its romantic associations with the gentility of the antebellum years. Well into the late 20th century, Georgia architects Edward Vason Jones of Albany and William Frank McCall, Jr., of Moultrie continued Southern traditions after most of their peers had succumbed to the lure of modernism.

Unlike the Georgian and Spanish Colonial revivals that filled 1920s suburbs across the country, the Anglo-Caribbean plantation house style never developed a national following. Instead, it remained rooted in the Old South, where the trappings of piazzas and pavilion roofs were added to 20th-century suburban homes as grace notes. Today, there is a resurgent interest in Southern traditions practiced by a new school of architects, many based in Atlanta like Historical Concepts, who take pride in reviving the story of antebellum plantations in designs for new old houses.

TELLING DETAIL

GREEK REVIVAL DORMERS

Most dormer windows are built too short and wide to be authentic. The Greek Revival dormers on Langford House are barely wider than their window sash, with side walls that fit snugly against the window casings. Enclosed by trim classical pilasters at the sides and a triangular pediment for the roof, the tall, narrow proportions of these diminutive Greek temples look just right.

Part of a school of 1920s traditional architects who reinvigorated the southern plantation house tradition, Atlanta architect Lewis Edmund Crook, Jr. (1898–1967) was among the best, as shown in his design for the L. E. Grant House (1948) in Buckhead.

The romantic charm of Langford House's southern piazza is evident as an inviting perch from which to watch evening sunsets.

Magnolia Mound Plantation

More West Indies-style plantations are preserved in Louisiana than in any other state. Many of these homes were not built by Frenchmen but by other European immigrants. Magnolia Mound Plantation, a historic house in Baton Rouge, shares the style of Langford House and offers a precedent with telling details of plantation house design.

Begun in 1786, Magnolia Mound is more French Colonial than Langford House, although it was built by Irishman John Joyce from County Cork, Ireland. The house illustrates how the regional vernacular of the West Indies was adopted in America by new European immigrants. Its hipped pavilion roof and pairs of French doors opening onto a piazza are classic features of the West Indies style.

The house is raised aboveground on brick foundation piers. A pavilion roof covers the long rectangular floor plan and piazza without a change in slope. Originally a small three-room settler's house, Magnolia Mound was enlarged in the early 19th century by adding a formal dining room and two service rooms onto the back. Having one of the earliest coved ceilings in the Mississippi Valley, the interiors were updated in Federal style in the 1950s.

The West Indies style of Magnolia Mound Plantation (1786), a historic house in Baton Rouge, Louisiana, provides a precedent for the plantation house details of Langford House.

(far left) The coved ceiling in the main parlor is one of the earliest in the Mississippi Valley. The cove is made of boards shaped into a curve over a wooden frame, beneath a ceiling of flat boards.

(left) The master bedroom was part of the original plantation house, constructed with beamed ceilings and heart pine floors now well worn with a dark amber patina of age.

(below) Pairs of French doors open onto a classic piazza that wraps the house on three sides. Double-hung windows were added in an early 19th-century alteration.

CHARLESTON SINGLE HOUSE

*"All Artificers, as Carpenters, Wheelwrights, Joyners, Coopers, Bricklayers, Smiths,
or diligent Husbandmen and Labourers, that are willing to advance their fortunes, and live in a most
pleasant healthful and beautiful Country…may take notice, that . . . they have made a Town,
called Charles-Town, where there is plenty of as rich ground as any in the world."*
—ROBERT HORNE, *A Brief Description of the Province of Carolina* (1666)

By the middle of the 18th century, Charleston was the wealthiest city in America. Founded in 1670, the city had become the principal port and market town for the Carolina colony. Merchant ships departed Charleston's docks daily, bringing crops of rice and indigo across the sea to England. Enriched by trade, the new plantation aristocracy of the Carolina Low Country created a metropolis filled with Georgian townhouses and all the trappings of tasteful English life.

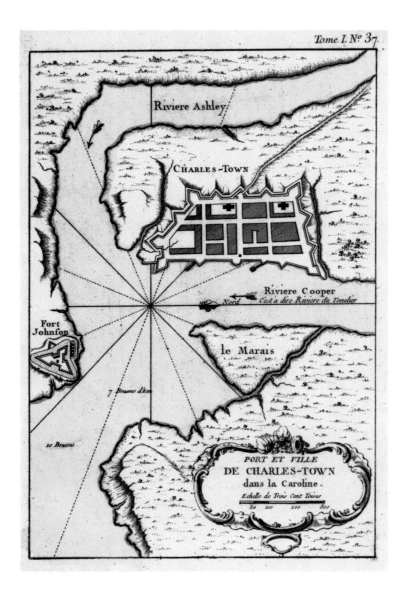

Riviere Ashley.

CHARLES-TOWN

Riviere Cooper
Nord   C'est a dire Riviere du Tonelier

Fort
Johnfon

le Marais

7 Braces d'Eau

10 Braces

PORT ET VILLE
DE CHARLES-TOWN
dans la Caroline.
Echelle de Trois Cent Toises
50   100   200   300

First settled in 1670, Charles Town was reestablished in 1680 on its present peninsular site between the Ashley and Cooper rivers as the principal port of the Carolina colony. The city was renamed Charleston in 1783.

FROM PLANTATIONS TO CLASSICAL CITY

The Carolina colony began in 1663 when a grateful King Charles II, restored to the English throne, bestowed the land below Virginia on eight Lords Proprietors for their faithful support. The most fervent promoter of the colony, Anthony Ashley-Cooper, Lord Shaftesbury, encouraged his fellow English peers to carve plantations from Carolina's tidewater estuaries. Among them were Sir John Colleton and a band of English planters from Barbados, who departed to seek their fortunes in Carolina's fertile soils.

Trade was the lifeblood of Charleston, bringing extraordinary wealth and the latest architectural styles to the city. Her seafaring merchants plied the triangle trade between England, Africa, and the West Indies, shipping barrels of rice and indigo to Europe and returning with molasses from the Caribbean and African slaves to work the plantations.

The classic homes of Charleston and the unique city plan of neighboring Savannah inspired architect Donald Rattner in his design for the new village of McAllister Point at The Ford Plantation in coastal Georgia. Much like the historic urban squares of Savannah, the Point is a neighborhood of townhouses built around a common green. On one of the neighborhood's deep, narrow lots, the architect has created a new three-story-tall home adorned with elegant piazzas in a spirited reinvention of the hallmark style of Charleston architecture—the Charleston single house.

In London, Charleston's merchant traders were dazzled by the architecture of Sir Christopher Wren and his followers, who had transformed the city after the Great Fire of 1666. They returned to Charleston carrying chests full of English pattern books illustrating the classical columns, porticos, and pediments they had seen in London. Soon English craftsmen sailed for the new colony to fill the demand for traditional trades, advertising their skills as masons, carpenters, cabinetmakers, and "draughtsman of houses" in the *South Carolina Gazette.*

By 1750 an enlightened city of Georgian churches, theaters, libraries, and elegant townhouses began to take shape on the Ashley and Cooper rivers. Charleston became the fourth largest city in America, after Philadelphia, Boston, and New York, and by far the richest. New Englander Josiah Quincy was starstruck by his visit: "In grandeur, splendour of buildings, decorations…and indeed in almost everything, it far surpasses all I ever saw in America!"

THE CHARLESTON SINGLE HOUSE

The Charleston single house was born in the opening years of the 18th century and would become the signature style of the city. The style is named for a floor plan that is only a single room deep to promote cross ventilation. Tall and slender, often three stories in height, the single house is offset to one side of its lot, with a narrow facade that faces the street and a long, formal front that faces a private sideyard.

In early Charleston, the sideyard between adjacent houses was a workplace, a long, narrow outdoor space containing a carriageway, a vegetable garden, and even a few cows and chickens. In later years, this space was transformed into an elegant formal garden, providing gracious outdoor living space. Behind the house were a separate office and kitchen, a "necessary," and perhaps a carriage house, with servants' quarters above the outbuildings.

The Charleston single house is the city's architectural trademark. Its proportions are tall, narrow, and deep, with the narrow end facing the street and the long front facing a private sideyard. Offset to one side of its lot, a two-story piazza *overlooks the sideyard garden.*

(above left) Charleston townhouses were decorated in the latest architectural styles imported from Georgian London, brought back to the city by merchant traders via English pattern books that illustrated classical details.

(above right) A two-story piazza *is the telling detail of a single house, its porches stacked one above the other and running down the long side of the house so that all rooms have access to the outdoors.*

The crown jewel of the single house is its two-story piazza, a double porch that runs down the length of the long side, sheltering doors and windows from the sun and providing relief from the hot, humid climate. Typically, piazza floors are stacked one above the other so that all rooms have access to a porch. Before air-conditioning, the piazza served as a cool outdoor sleeping area, with shutter panels between the columns for privacy.

Although Charleston's classicism came from London, the single house had its roots in the West Indies. Beginning in the 1680s, Englishmen from Barbados imported the design concept of a long, narrow house to draw breezes through the interiors, sowing the seeds of Anglo-Caribbean design in the city. This Caribbean model was well suited to the humid climate of the Carolinas and found a compatible home in Charleston, where lot proportions were slender and deep, typically 40 ft. to 50 ft. wide by 80 ft. to 120 ft. deep.

The concept of a narrow and deep townhouse was imported from Barbados by English planters in the 1680s. The oldest stone house in Charleston, the Pink House, was built in the 1690s of West Indies coral stone that had a natural pink cast.

(top right) The historic Battery on the point overlooking the Ashley and Cooper rivers is lined with some of the most elegant single houses in Old and Historic Charleston.

The single house and its practical piazza became Charleston's stock-in-trade. Today, glorious rows of well-preserved single houses line the streets of Old and Historic Charleston from The Battery to The Citadel.

A SINGLE HOUSE ON GEORGIA'S COAST

For those who know Charleston, the source of Donald Rattner's design for his new single house at McAllister Point is unmistakable. He pays tribute to the city's late 18th-century classical period, borrowing architecture from historic single houses without copying them, a process of inspiration and interpretation that is the hallmark of new old houses.

Like the trademark houses of Charleston, the Rattner house sits right next to the sidewalk. It is narrow and deep, standing three stories tall above a ground floor of handmade bricks. The upper floors are cream-colored stucco, like Charleston's early stucco-covered houses painted in pastel shades of yellow, pink, green, and blue. The long side of the house carries a double piazza that catches sea breezes rolling across Georgia's coastal salt marshes.

As its name implies, the floor plan of a single house is slender and deep. Its rooms are arranged in a single row from front to back, with doors opening out to a piazza.

In his design, Rattner uses classical ornamental details to define significant features and make the simple stucco walls come to life. Elaborate curved pediments on top of the first-floor windows cast strong shadows and give the windows prominence. On the second floor, the window pediments are shallow, blocky lintels of lesser importance, while on the third floor there are none. And on top of the house, a deep cornice overhangs the roof like a crown that caps the wall at the skyline.

The stucco walls rest on brick foundations, mirroring another Charleston building tradition. Early houses were raised up on sturdy brick walls to protect them from damp soils and flooding. The ground floors were used only for kitchens, workrooms, and storage spaces of little value, while the floors above held more precious living rooms and bedrooms. Resurrecting the custom, Rattner designed the ground floor of the new house for the garage, utilities, and storage rooms that can be sacrificed when the water rises.

Handsome brick piers and iron gates frame the entrance to many of Charleston's historic landmarks. The stairs up to the McAllister Point house were inspired by this tradition, winding through a wrought-iron gate hung on classical brick piers. Iron handrails trace the stairs up to a front-door landing that is paved in a checkerboard of gray and white marble.

The architect designed the traditional street doorway based on classic Charleston models, an exterior door opening onto a porch that is unique to the city's single houses. His mahogany door and its fanlight window fit neatly inside a decorative cornice and brackets. The door opens onto a broad piazza, authentic in every detail, where a row of stout Doric columns supports the second-floor porch.

(opposite page) Donald Rattner's new Charleston single house is three stories tall, its cream-colored stucco walls sitting on a raised brick foundation. A double piazza attached to the long side overlooks Georgia's coastal wetlands.

(far left) A master bedroom and living room wing sits on the back of the house, with its own porch looking out to the salt marshes.

(left) Constructed of new hand-made bricks with decorative accents such as an oval window, the ground floor of the new house recalls the Carolina tidewater tradition of building raised foundation walls to protect the principal rooms from damp soils and flooding.

Opening into a small entrance foyer from the piazza, the front door is a simple sash-and-panel door surrounded by sidelights and a transom window.

CHARLESTON STREET DOOR

What appears to be the front door to a Charleston single house is in fact a street door that opens onto one end of the piazza. The real front door into the house is located halfway down the porch, where it enters into the middle of the house. Because the piazza is often raised well above the street, a stairway leads from the sidewalk to the street door.

Rooms all in a row

The main front door is halfway down the piazza. It is modest compared with the street doorway, a design of simple glass panels that opens into a small foyer. The floor plan is a string of rooms arranged en suite—lined up in a row from front to back—like the plan of all early Charleston single houses. The library spans the front of the house; the kitchen and stair hall fill the middle; and the dining and living rooms are toward the back. All are one room deep and have windows on both sides to draw cross ventilation through the house.

The piazza that opens through the street door is framed by a row of Doric columns with a balustrade of turned spindles running between them. Gas lanterns hang from a ceiling of coffered panels, a classic woodworking detail found on old tidewater porches from Charleston to Savannah.

The library is the most refined room in the house, its four walls paneled in antique longleaf heart pine. One of the prized wood species used for colonial millwork, heart pine was chosen for floors, paneling, and trim as well as for structural posts and beams. Unfortunately, by the early 20th century so much longleaf pine had been harvested that now all the old growth is gone.

Stair halls of single houses usually divided the long floor plan in half across the middle. In the McAllister Point house, the stairway spirals upstairs through walls decorated with a mural depicting a tidewater landscape. Such hand-painted murals often graced Southern homes, painted by itinerant artists who roamed the countryside in search of commissions. Here the mural is a reminder of the traditions that have shaped this new old Charleston single house.

OLD AND HISTORIC CHARLESTON

Most of the oldest architecture of Charleston has been lost. A catastrophic fire raged through the city in 1740, destroying half of the original town and most of the early houses made of wood. After two more devastating fires, many Charlestonians rebuilt their wooden houses in bricks made of red-brown tidewater clay. To protect the soft Carolina bricks from humidity, they were coated with stucco and often etched with a pattern of lines to look like stone, a technique called scoring.

Several surviving historic houses reveal the heritage of Barbados in Charleston. The oldest house influenced by the West Indies, the Robert Brewton House of 1730, is tall and narrow with louvered shutters to protect the windows in hurricane season. On the second floor, a small iron balcony overlooks the street, a detail adapted from the street balconies of Spanish Colonial architecture.

(opposite page) An antique grandfather clock holds court at the top of the stairs, a sentinel that ties the new old house to its colonial roots.

(far left) The refined Georgian raised-panel walls in the library are made of antique heart pine, a prized wood for colonial millwork, making this the most sophisticated room in the house.

(left) The kitchen is conveniently located off the entrance foyer. It is designed for today's lifestyle with all of the amenities trimly fit into traditional painted cabinetry with glass-front cabinets and unlacquered brass bin pull hardware.

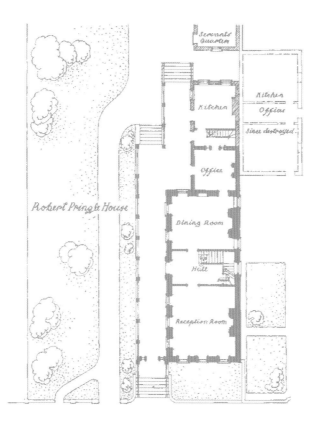

The Charleston single house is named for a floor plan that is arranged in a string of rooms lined up in a row from front to back. A traditional single house is one room wide and two or three rooms deep, with a stair hall that divides the house through the middle across from the main front door. Most rooms have windows on both sides to draw cross ventilation through the interior and a door that opens onto the piazza.

After a devastating fire in 1740 wiped out many early wooden houses in Charleston, new homes, such as the William Vanderhorst House (1740), were built in soft Carolina bricks plastered with a protective stucco covering. Its front door opening directly onto the street was typical for single houses before piazzas came into vogue.

Clapboard facades on single houses were often decorated with classical trimmings such as decorative window lintels, pilaster corners, and projected roof cornices, as seen on the house of botanist Thomas Lamboll (1739).

Most early houses did not have piazzas, which were often added later onto West Indies-style homes. The plain stucco walls of the William Vanderhorst House (1740) show a single house before the distinctive Charleston feature was introduced. Single-story piazzas began to appear in 1700, but double piazzas were not common until the 1750s. The clapboard house of botanist Thomas Lamboll (1739) has a traditional piazza as well as an elaborate street doorway that records the fashionable good taste of the owner.

The double house

Charleston's most bountiful years began in the 1760s after the French and Indian War, when the streets filled with Georgian single houses built in clapboard, brick, and stucco. By the time the Revolutionary War began in 1775, wealthy traders such as Miles Brewton and William Gibbes had brought another architectural tradition to Charleston from Georgian London—the double house.

Illogical as it may seem, the double house is not two single houses joined together, but a center-hall Georgian built on a wide building lot. The lineage of the double house derives from the work of English architects Robert Adam, James Gibbs, and William Chambers, whose fashionable classical townhouses filled early 18th-century London. The Brewton and Gibbes houses have symmetrical facades facing the street and ornamental porticos framing the front door. More like plantation houses than townhouses, both are surrounded by formal gardens and rows of outbuildings, adding Georgian opulence to Charleston's streets.

The entry foyer and stair hall cut through the middle of the house, with a staircase on the back wall that winds its way upstairs through mural-covered walls that depict a tidewater landscape.

Single House Reborn

Unlike many colonial styles of architecture, the single house stayed at home in Charleston, perhaps a reflection of its unique roots and the proportions of the city's building lots. Despite the worldliness of its citizens, the style hardly traveled elsewhere, even to nearby Savannah, founded in 1733, where a similar climate and riverside location would have made it work well.

Shortly after the American Revolution, the single house did find a new home, but it was offshore. Loyalists to the English Crown fled the Carolinas for expatriate colonies on the British islands of Bermuda and the Bahamas, where they built familiar homes with piazzas, returning the single house style to its Anglo-Caribbean roots.

The single house remained unique to Charleston until New Urbanist architects rediscovered its design potential in recent times. The narrow lots of traditional neighborhood developments—towns designed on New Urbanist principles—are ideal settings for houses that are slender and deep but provide plenty of outdoor living on porches.

Single houses have found their place in the new Low Country communities of Newpoint, I'On, and Habersham. There, traditional developers Vincent Graham and Robert Turner have reinterpreted the spirit of the single house in imaginative variations, combining inspiration from the historic towns of Beaufort, Charleston, and Savannah to create new neighborhoods. The compelling features of a single house turned with its narrow end to the street and piazzas on the long side work as well now as they did in the past.

During Charleston's most prosperous years, another architectural tradition, the double house, was introduced. A double house is a center-hall Georgian with rooms laid out symmetrically behind a formal facade and entrance portico, as on the William Gibbes House (1772).

A streetscape in the new traditional town of Newpoint, South Carolina, shows how the single house and its piazza work well in a New Urbanist setting where building lots are narrow and deep, reviving the spirit of Low Country outdoor living in the 21st century.

MILES BREWTON HOUSE

Completed in 1769, Miles Brewton House is the quintessential example of a Charleston double house, a center-hall design sharing architectural features with nearby Drayton Hall.

Brewton was an architectural dilettante whose personal library included a dozen volumes on the building arts. He hired Ezra Waite, a self-described "Civil Architect, Housebuilder in general, and Carver from London," to draw up the plans and supervise construction. Like most housewrights in America at the time, Waite relied on English pattern books to design plans and elevations, copy decorative details, and calculate the correct proportions for classical columns.

The Brewton House is a symmetrical design shaped like a cube, a Palladian motif that Thomas Jefferson also used for the Rotunda at the University of Virginia. The walls are made of brick laid in Flemish bond beneath a hipped roof. Its centerpiece is a refined two-story portico with a double porch of classical columns supporting a pediment. The exquisite craftsmanship and carving of the portico represent a level of skill unsurpassed anywhere in 18th-century colonial America.

4

OUR CONTINENTAL HERITAGE

FREE TRADE, LOG CABINS, AND BROTHERLY LOVE

"The first planters in these parts were the Dutch, and soon after them the Swedes and Finns. The Dutch applied themselves to traffic, the Swedes and Finns to husbandry."

—WILLIAM PENN, *A Letter from William Penn, Proprietary and Governor of Pennsylvania in America* (1683)

Spain, France, and England were not the only players in the European power struggle eager to establish colonies in the New World. In the 17th century, the other Continental powers of Sweden and the Netherlands emerged to challenge their dominance by setting up footholds in the Americas. Although the Dutch and Swedish colonies were short-lived, they opened the floodgates of European emigration to the New World. By the early 18th century, William Penn was welcoming waves of German, Swiss, and Scots-Irish émigrés to populate his new colony and fill the land with house styles remembered from the Old Country.

Now reconstructed at the Frontier Culture Museum in Staunton, Virginia, the German Farm was built in the 1600s and originally stood in the village of Hördt in the Rhineland. From the Rhineland came many of Pennsylvania's German immigrants who became known as the "Pennsylvania Dutch."

The Dutch: Brick, Stone, and Shingles

English navigator Henry Hudson first saw the river that bears his name while sailing for Holland in 1609. From the deck of the *Halve Maen,* Hudson laid Dutch claim to the Atlantic shore from the Connecticut River to the Delaware and up the Hudson as far north as Albany. The Dutch founded New Netherland in 1624, but after only four decades ceded the colony to the English, who renamed it New York.

The Dutch started New Amsterdam on Manhattan Island, where they left a legacy of enterprise, tolerance, and celebration that shaped the cosmopolitan character of future New York. Founded by the Dutch West India Company, the town was settled by men of commerce who traded freely around the globe. Unlike their doctrinaire Puritan counterparts in New England, the Dutch embraced a cross culture of newcomers from French Huguenots and Flemish Walloons to Englishmen, Africans, and Jews.

The Dutch imported late medieval house styles from the streets of Amsterdam and the farms of Holland and Flanders. Soon the urban centers of New York and Albany were built like Dutch towns, with winding streets, canals, and brick townhouses graced with stepped gables, steep roofs, and patterned brickwork. Along the upper Hudson where limestone was plentiful, Dutch and Huguenot farmers built houses of stone rather than brick, laying up fieldstone walls over a timber frame of H-shaped posts and beams. On Dutch farms in western Long Island and northern New Jersey, they built houses that were covered with shingles or weatherboards and often mixed with walls of red sandstone.

The winding streets of New York and Albany were filled with Dutch Colonial townhouses imitating those in Amsterdam, Utrecht, and Leiden. Prosperous Dutch merchants built their houses with the familiar steep roofs, crow-stepped gables, and patterned brickwork of the Low Countries.

In the 17th century, New Amsterdam was a cosmopolitan center of commerce and world trade.

The Van Jean is an unusually well arranged Dutch Colonial house. It has many special features not generally found in houses of this price. It has a charming entrance that gives an atmosphere of welcome. It has Colonial cottage windows with divided lights above and on light below. Add to this the white siding and contrasting red or green roof with the red brick chimney and you have a home that is sure to charm the most critical.

The interior is deeply planned. While it has the latest conveniences, its price is unusually low. Why? Because of careful planning and no wasted space. If a buyer of this size wants with your requirements, you will make no mistake in selecting the Van Jean.

FIRST FLOOR

The Recreation Hall. Enter upon the spacious hall reveals the extended character of this Dutch Colonial home. An open stairway leads to the second floor. To the left of stairway is a coat closet with pole for wraps and a hat rack, accommodating a large number of guests. A telephone table which may be set along the left wall. On each side of this spacious hall are wide, generous with French doors, making it possible to enjoy the full dining room and the dining room on the summer side.

The Living Room. To the right of hall you enter the living room, which is of the utmost proportions to screen exterior in furnishings to give best advantage. It is unusually large, so the size of French doors. The living room plan is an attractive feature with their nice opening out. French doors to a brick eaten and fireplace which is the center of attention. One can entertain your sitting, as the porch is ready. Windows or flower effect afford plenty of light and air, making a cheery room.

The Sun Room. A French door opens into the sun room from the living room if French is referred. Seven large windows that make the large living room and the dining room on the summer side.

What Our Prices Include

At the prices quoted we will furnish all the material to build this six-room colonial house, consisting of:

Lumber: Lath	
Roofing: Oriental Slate Surfaced Shingles: Guaranteed for 17 years.	
Siding: Cedar Clear Cypress or Clear Red Cedar Bevel Siding.	
Framing Lumber: No. 1 Quality Douglas Fir or Pacific Coast Hemlock.	
Flooring: ... inch Clear Oak throughout; two of Kitchen and Bathroom which are ... inch Clear Maple.	
Trim: Casing, Clear Grade Douglas Fir or Pacific Coast Hemlock.	
Finishing Lumber: High Grade Millwork (see pages 100 and 101).	
Interior Doors: One-Panel Soft-Frame Design of Clear Fir.	
Trim: Birch Hard Plane, of Beautiful Grain Douglas Fir or Yellow Pine, Built-Stair Treads, Nosed and Rail.	
Mantel: Seat.	
Kitchen Cabinets: Medicine Case.	
Windows of California Clear White Pine.	
Heavy Waterproof Building Paper; Sash Weights.	
Eaves Trough and Down Spout.	
Hardware (see pages 103, 104 and 105).	
Paint for Three Coats Outside Trim and Siding.	
Fine-Coat Enamel Finish for Trim, Mahogany Stain, Shellac, Varnish and Paint for Interior Trim.	
Wood Filler and Varnish.	
Wood Filler and Two Coats of Varnish for Oak Floors.	
Two Coats of Varnish for Maple Floors.	
Complete Plans and Specifications.	
Built up a concrete and brick foundation and excavated under the entire house.	
We guarantee enough material to build this house. Prices do not include cement, brick or plaster.	
See illustration of "Honor Bilt" houses on pages 12 and 13.	

OPTIONS

Solid Oak Oriental Asphalt Slate Surface Strip Shingles, guaranteed for seventeen years, instead of wood shingles.	
For $P2587A add $59.00 and for $P2587A-add $3.00 for this house.	
Wood Plaster and Plaster Finish, in tint the place of common lath, add 1/4 per cent, $256.00; without sun room, $247.00 extra. See page 140.	
Screens, front and storm, with sun room, $93.00 extra; without sun room, $71.00.	
Storm Doors and 17 inches galvanized pipe with sun room, $12.00 extra; without sun room, $44.00.	
For prices of Plumbing, Heating, Wiring, Electric Fixtures and Shades see pages 138 and 139.	

The Dining Room. To the left of the hall is the dining room. It is of good size. Windows on two sides give the desired light and ventilation.

The Kitchen. From the dining room you pass a swinging door into the model kitchen. Here the sink, the kitchen cabinet, the pantry closet and space for stove and table have been arranged with a thought to save the housewife too many steps as possible. A high casement window gives plenty of light over the range and sink. The four under provides space for an ice box, which can be iced without leaving the kitchen floor. To the right are stairs leading to the basement and to the left is the grade door to yard.

The Bedrooms. The stairway hall has a coat and other window to the landing. A short flight connects with all bedrooms and bath. Our side on the main bedroom of large size with accommodations. Two clothes closets are at one of each room. Between the rooms and underneath window is a built-in seat, arranged which provide light and furniture and light are agreeable to the various apartments of windows in each room. Closet to the bedroom and laundry to the bathroom from the second floor hall.

The Basement. Room for furnace, laundry and storage.
Height of Ceilings. Basement, 7 feet high from floor to joists, with cement floor. First floor, 9 feet from floor to ceiling. Second floor, 8 feet 7 inches from floor to ceiling.

Can be built on a lot 40 feet wide with sun room, and on a lot 40 feet wide without sun room.

This house can be built with the rooms reversed. See page 3.

FIRST FLOOR PLAN | **SECOND FLOOR PLAN**

For Our Easy Payment Plan See Page 144—For Our Information Blank See Page 141
Page 30 *See Interior Views of The Van Jean Home on opposite Page*

The Van Jean
"Already Cut" and Fitted
P2587A Price with Sun Room, $2,887.00
P2587B Price without Sun Room . . $2,636.00

DUTCH COLONIAL REVIVAL

※

The style we think of today as Dutch Colonial wasn't really Dutch. It evolved from a hybrid of ethnic traditions in areas settled by the English, Scots-Irish, and French Huguenots along with the Dutch. This mix of cultural roots brought us the shingled homes with gambrel roofs, shed dormers, and flared eaves that we now mistakenly call "Dutch Colonial." This style became popular for suburban houses in early 20th-century home-plan catalogs such as Sears, Roebuck and Co.'s *Modern Homes.*

THE SWEDISH: SCANDINAVIAN LOG CABINS

Seventeenth-century Sweden was a major European power, a kingdom that included parts of Norway, all of Finland, a slice of Russia, as well as the Baltic countries. In a direct challenge to the Dutch, the New Sweden Company engaged Peter Minuit, former governor of New Netherland, to colonize the western shore of Delaware Bay. Minuit founded New Sweden in 1638 at Fort Christina, which later became the city of Wilmington.

Over the next 17 years, some 600 Swedes and Finns settled in forts and small farms on both banks of the Delaware in an attempt to seal the river against Dutch and English intruders. They established Indian trading posts for furs and tobacco as far north as the future site of Philadelphia. The Swedish presence was small and disorganized, however. With only meager support from home and limited weapons, the colony became

The lasting legacy of New Sweden was the introduction of the Scandinavian log cabin to the New World. For the next three centuries, stacked-log construction became the favored building type for pioneer homes across the American frontier.

easy prey for Dutch ships under the command of Peter Stuyvesant, who conquered New Sweden in 1655.

While their tenure was short, the Swedish left a permanent mark on American building, for it was the Swedes who introduced the Scandinavian log cabin to the New World. Constructed of stacked logs notched at their corners and chinked with mud, the log house became the iconic frontier dwelling of America. Quick and easy shelter, a log house could be built by unskilled hands using available materials, but it was often cold and drafty. Yet when William Penn arrived from England to found Pennsylvania, he was so taken with the Swedish log cabin that he promoted it as his "beginner's house" for new settlers.

The Pennsylvania Dutch: Quaker Town and German Country

In 1681 William Penn was granted a charter from King Charles II of England to a tract of land west of the Delaware River as his "sylvania" for oppressed English Quakers. With its code of tolerance and brotherly love, the Pennsylvania colony welcomed Europeans of all religions and creeds fleeing persecution and poverty. Soon Quakers, Amish, Baptists, and Mennonites flocked to the Delaware Valley. Joining them were Scots-Irish exiles as well as impoverished Swiss and German farmers from the provinces of Saxony, the Rhineland, and the Black Forest. Within five years, there were more than 9,000 new Pennsylvanians.

The rock-strewn soils of the fertile river valleys around Philadelphia provided raw material for German, English Quaker, and Scots-Irish settlers to build solid fieldstone houses with oak floor beams and roof rafters, a style that became the classic Pennsylvania Dutch farmhouse.

The early 1700s Irish Farm reconstructed at the Frontier Culture Museum in Staunton, Virginia, originally stood in County Tyrone, Northern Ireland, a region traditionally known as Ulster, from which thousands of Scots-Irish emigrated to America.

(opposite page and below) Pennsylvania's Hans Herr House, which dates to 1719, is an iconic example of an early German fieldstone farmhouse.

While the Quaker Society of Friends settled comfortably into urban Philadelphia, German peasant farmers gravitated toward the rich farmland of the surrounding countryside. Known as the "Pennsylvania Dutch"—an English corruption of the German word *Deutsch*—they started farms and cottage industries on the rural frontier. In the Brandywine and Schuylkill River valleys, the Germans built faithful reproductions of the *flurkuchenhaus*, a three-room farmhouse typical of the Rhine Valley. As prosperity came, they built more permanent houses made of solid fieldstone that became the classic Pennsylvania Dutch farmhouse.

By the mid 18th century, the Scots-Irish and Germans of Pennsylvania, looking for cheaper land, had transported the fieldstone farmhouse down the foothills of the Appalachians, through the Valley of Virginia, and into the Carolinas. As their building traditions merged with those of the English colonies, they invented the classic I-house, a simple two-story wooden farmhouse that became a favorite in rural America.

In the opening decades of the 19th century, these Appalachian highlanders pushed their way farther south along the Natchez Trace into the Republic of Texas. Welcomed by Stephen Austin, they settled into his colony of San Felipe de Austin, bringing their building traditions of log and fieldstone to the frontier of the Southwest borderlands.

SWEDISH LOG CABIN

"Queen Christina renounced, in favor of the Swedes, all claims and pretensions the English had in that country . . . The first colony was set off, and Peter Menuet was placed over it, . . . setting sail from Gothenburg in a ship of war, called the Kalmar Nickel, laden with people, provisions, ammunition and merchandise suitable for traffic and gifts to the Indians."
—REVEREND ISRAEL ACRELIUS, *Account of the Swedish in New Sweden* (1759)

Every American knows that Abraham Lincoln grew up in a log cabin, the symbol of our humble roots. We are taught that the log cabin was a homegrown frontier invention, but that turns out to be a myth. Instead, the idea arrived in America with Swedish colonists who planted a short-lived colony on the Delaware River. For the next three centuries, the Swedish log cabin spread from Pennsylvania to Texas and over the Rockies as the iconic frontier dwelling.

The New Sweden colony was founded along the shores of the lower Delaware River, a disputed area that the Dutch of New Netherland considered part of their New World colony, later incorporated into Pennsylvania.

High up in the Ruby River Valley of southwestern Montana, a salvaged early 20th-century log schoolhouse has been re-created as a mountain retreat by architect Candace Tillotson-Miller. Her Ruby River Cabin is a distant cousin of America's early Swedish log houses, its rough-hewn squared logs, dovetailed corners, and clay chinking unchanged since pioneer times.

THE LOG CABIN MYTH

Log cabins are the most revered of all American house types. Legend has it that English colonists began to build with logs as soon as they arrived in the New World, but the English had no log-building experience in their homeland, nor did early Spanish, Dutch, or French settlers. While the French adopted upright log construction for their first homes in Acadia, they set logs vertically in the ground rather than horizontally, like the stockades of a frontier fort.

True stacked-log building was introduced by the Swedes who came to America in the early 17th century. After decades of overpopulation and poor soils at home, Swedish peasant farmers left the provinces of Dalarna and Värmland and transported centuries-old Scandinavian log construction to the New World. Although the colony of New Sweden lasted only 17 years, the Swedes left a permanent legacy of homebuilding.

Short-Lived New Sweden

New Sweden was founded in 1638 when former Dutch governor Peter Minuit, hired by the New Sweden Company to develop the fur trade, sailed into Delaware Bay to start a colony at Fort Christina (present-day Wilmington). Within five years, the Swedes had gained a toehold and fortified their grip by founding Fort Elfsborg on the New Jersey side of the Delaware River. From there they expanded settlement northward in small farms and Indian trading posts, always wary of Dutch threats from New Netherland to the north.

They were right to be worried, for the Dutch believed that their colony included the Delaware, a boundary known to them as the South River. Soon the hot-tempered governor of New Amsterdam, Peter Stuyvesant, had suffered enough Swedish humiliation. In 1655 he sent a fleet of ships to reclaim the Dutch territory, and realizing that resistance would be futile,

What became the classic American log cabin was virtually unknown to the Spanish, Dutch, and English. While the French used upright log building in Acadia, the Swedes were the first to use stacked-log construction with logs laid horizontally and crossed at the corners.

Scandinavian Log Cabin

The Swedish log cabin traces its roots to the medieval *stugas* of Scandinavia. Most of these early single-story cottages were made of logs or hewn planks, often beneath a thick roof of sod for insulation. The centerpiece was a large stove room called a *stuga*. The stuga had a two-sided fireplace built into one corner. In addition, there was a *forstuga*, a small room that served as an entry hall, and a *kammara* that was a bedchamber. This three-room arrangement remained essentially unchanged in American log cabins.

LOG CORNER NOTCHES

The most distinctive feature of log construction is the corner notch, cut into the ends of logs to make them stack firmly in place. The most common types are the saddle notch, the V-notch, and the half-dovetail. The saddle notch is most familiar, where round logs overlap with their ends projecting at the corners, like Lincoln Logs®. In a V-notch (top below), each log is cut on its top and bottom edge with male and female Vs that mate when stacked. The complex half-dovetail notch (bottom below) is saw-cut in the shape of a bird's tail and angled so that two overlapped corners lock in a rigid joint, each slanted so that rainwater drains out of the joint.

Governor Johan Risingh and his outnumbered Swedes surrendered without a shot. But Dutch control did not last long, for the colony was turned over to England only nine years later.

When Englishman William Penn received his charter for Pennsylvania in 1681, his lands included the three Delaware counties of New Sweden. Penn became a devoted fan of the Swedish log cabin and so admired its practical system for building homes quickly that he urged his European immigrants to follow the Swedish plan. English Quakers, German Rhinelanders, and Scots-Irish eagerly took Penn's advice as they settled into log cabins in the countryside around Philadelphia.

A QUICK AND EASY HOME

Penn's plan for a log house followed the Swedish model exactly, with walls of stacked logs covered by a gable roof of long split shingles. It could be built by unskilled

Ruby River Cabin is a salvaged early 20th-century log schoolhouse that has been re-created as a mountain retreat in the highlands of the Medina River Valley in southwestern Montana.

Hewn log cabins were the pioneer dwelling of choice for frontier Americans migrating across the Midwestern plains and into the Rocky Mountains, where the Swedish tradition survived into the early 20th century.

hands using a common broadax and assembled with little help. Large trees were plentiful across the American frontier, making logs a natural by-product of clearing the land for cultivation. Easy to build using readily available materials, log cabins caught on like wildfire with early settlers.

Not everyone admired the early American log cabin. One visitor whined that "the miserable dwellings of this place consist of logs piled one above the other with mud and moss to fill up the crevices."

Round logs chinked with clay leaked cold air and were hard to keep dry as green lumber shrank and swelled with the seasons. The logs would inevitably rot when water collected in corner notches. These problems were solved by better methods of squaring hewn logs and cutting dovetail corners to drain off rainwater. Hewn log cabins then became the pioneer dwelling of choice for frontier Americans, changing little as they migrated across mountains and plains for the next three centuries.

Early Swedish log cabins were made of stacked oak logs under roofs of hand-split shingles. They were quickly and easily built by unskilled colonists using a common broadax and assembled with the help of willing neighbors.

(left) The Early Plank House in Lewes, Delaware, is a surviving example of the early houses of New Sweden. Possibly used as a dwelling or as slave quarters, the house has notched plank walls that were common in log building in 1740s Delaware.

A Rocky Mountain Schoolhouse

The reconstructed Ruby River Cabin started life as a frontier schoolhouse built in a high valley settled after Montana's gold rush of 1863. Architect Candace Tillotson-Miller uprooted the old schoolhouse and reset its well-preserved logs on new granite foundations, adding a few sympathetic changes such as a screened porch and shed-dormer roof.

The frontier-plain structure is a timeless survivor in this Big Sky valley. Its large hewn oak logs must have been harvested at a time when sturdy hardwoods were plentiful. Square-hewn logs like those used for Ruby River Cabin were an improvement on round logs because they could be stacked tightly together. Dovetail joints hold the logs in place where they overlap at the corners.

The long logs used for the roof beams of the cabin project beyond the face of the gable ends by several feet:

one at the ridge line, one at the midpoint of the roof, and another at the eave line. The projecting beam ends are cut in a series of steps to make them decorative as well as structural, adding artistic flair to the job of carrying the eaves and roof rafters.

Chimneys and fireplaces were among the most difficult things for pioneers to build, but they were essential for cooking and warmth. The first chimneys were made of sticks formed into a primitive flue and coated with clay mortar. These early chimneys, called Welsh chimneys, were prone to catch fire, so in time they were replaced with stone and brick. Since skilled masons were in short supply in the outback, frontiersmen had to fend for themselves.

The cabin has been rebuilt as a fishing camp on the banks of the Ruby River, one of Montana's premier trout streams. The log cabin was lifted from its former site and moved onto new granite foundations, with additions for a screened porch and shed-dormer roof.

(opposite page) The rustic simplicity of log walls chinked with mortar colors the character of Ruby River Cabin. This relaxed mountain retreat blends rough-hewn plank floors with a fireplace built of granite blocks.

(opposite page) There is nothing fancy about the cookhouse kitchen of weathered barn boards with cabinets tucked into a corner off the living room.

(top left) Long log roof beams project beyond the face of the gable ends of the cabin by several feet. The ends are cut in a stepped profile that adds decorative detail to their rustic simplicity.

(top right) The original square-hewn hardwood logs were cut and carted from the hills surrounding the mountain valley. Dovetail notches hold the logs together where they overlap at the corners.

(left) Some interior beams have been left as round logs, while those that are squared show the telltale marks of being hewn with a broadax.

The new chimney at Ruby River Cabin shows the patient effort required of pioneers to fit rough stones into a structure of interlocking blocks. First, rocks had to be collected off nearby ledges, then hammered into roughly square chunks, hauled up ladders, and mortared in place with mud and sand. If you weren't good at it, the whole pile would tumble down before you were done.

Primitive preserved

Ruby River Cabin shares the classic three-room plan of an early Swedish log home. Since the cabin is a hunting and fishing lodge, the living room is open to the ceiling with trophies mounted on the walls. The log walls are treated just like the outside of the cabin, finished with sand-colored synthetic mortar chinking. Rough-sawn oak planks are used for floorboards,

which are fastened in place with square-cut nails hammered through the faces.

The kitchen resembles a primitive frontier cookhouse tucked off in one corner of the living room. The cabinets and plate racks are rough barn boards nailed together with their weather stains on display. In this small space, there is just enough room for one person to cook chow.

The same rough-hewn look is true of the bathroom, where the towel bars are branches on a tree stump. In one corner an old ceramic sink hangs off the log walls with no provision for counter space. The shower is a galvanized steel washtub hauled out of the barn with a hoop ring for a shower rod. As crude as these details may seem, they have been carefully crafted by Tillotson-Miller to preserve Ruby River Cabin as a rustic log cabin rather than a slick dude ranch.

On the back porch of the cabin, antique timber posts and beams frame picture-perfect views of the mountains of southwestern Montana's Big Sky country.

(above top) The front door to the cabin opens into a pocket-size vestibule.

(above bottom) Architect Tillotson-Miller had doors custom made from rough-sawn fir boards with the saw marks still showing, left unfinished to weather over time. One of the door handles is made of a curved birch tree branch, bark and all.

(left) The fireplace is intended to look pioneer handcrafted, with chunks of weathered granite that range in size from chips to boulders. The stones are laid up evenly in a dry-stacked pattern so that every stone edge shows. A thick stone slab caps the fireplace as a mantel shelf.

Throughout the Appalachian Mountains, log cabins have been preserved in national parks and living-history museums. In the mountain valleys of Tennessee and Kentucky, German and Scots-Irish pioneers blended their heritage of building in stone with the Scandinavian log cabin.

LOG CABINS OF APPALACHIA

Pockets of log cabin heritage survive in the Appalachian Mountains of Kentucky and Tennessee where log building persisted well into the 20th century. The mountains were a formidable barrier on the western edge of the 13 colonies that marked the first American frontier. Cheap land and unlimited freedom lay on the backside, but so did dangerous Indian Country, and only the intrepid dared cross the mountain passes to start a new life. The most determined among them were the Scots-Irish, who were followed into the Appalachian highlands by Rhineland Germans.

The homes built by these European settlers were almost uniformly log with stone foundations and chimneys, a marriage of Scandinavian log building with German and Scots-Irish stone traditions. The settlers hewed logs of oak, chestnut, and poplar averaging

A one-room log cabin with a stone chimney on the end was called a "single-pen" cabin (left). When two one-room cabins were built together under one roof, with an open porch between them, it was called a "dogtrot" (above). A "saddlebag" cabin was made by adding a new single-pen onto the chimney end of a one-room cabin, the two sharing a central chimney.

12 in. to 15 in. in diameter and 25 ft. to 30 ft. long into square timbers joined together with a dovetail notch—a clever Pennsylvania German innovation.

Early pioneer log cabins were often enlarged as the family grew. Space was added by attaching another cabin to the original one, transforming a single-pen cabin into a double-pen or a dogtrot with a covered porch or breezeway between them.

Influenced by the colonies of the English tidewater coast, Appalachian frontiersmen eventually built more formal two-story log houses with classic center-hall plans—two rooms joined by a central hallway and staircase. This form eventually became the Southern I-house, a two-story-tall farmhouse with a chimney at each end, a porch across the front and back, and often a rear addition for a kitchen ell. The I-house was simple and efficient to build, and in time it spread across America to become the quintessential Victorian wood-frame farmhouse.

In time the Appalachian log cabin became a more formal two-story house with a center-hall plan, as in the Thompson-Brown House (1820s). The Southern I-house emerged from this type as a classic two-story farmhouse with porches front and back and chimneys at each end.

JOHN OLIVER CABIN

❧

Many of the mountain homesteads of Appalachia are still well preserved within national parks and frontier museums. Typical of them is the John Oliver Cabin in Cades Cove, Tennessee, part of the Great Smoky Mountains National Park.

Staking their claim in 1826, John and Lurany Oliver were the first white settlers in Cades Cove, a wilderness Appalachian valley ringed by mountains. With little more than some seeds and a few tools, the Olivers set about carving a homestead out of the woods. John Oliver built his log cabin from hardwoods cut down while clearing the land. He constructed a traditional three-room plan with a massive chimney made of stacked fieldstones on the end wall.

In time Oliver added lean-to porches across the two long sides for covered outdoor storage and work areas. The first windows in his cabin were rough cutouts in the walls, but he later added glass window sash when such niceties could be purchased from tradesmen outside the valley. For more than a hundred years, the Oliver family lived in this primitive mountain home, eventually purchased by the National Park Service in 1934.

DUTCH COLONIAL REVIVAL

"The Dutch town had most of the evidence of its origin: the houses were nearly all constructed with their gables to the street, and were built of klinkers, small, hard, well burnt bricks imported from Holland. Every dwelling had its stoep, a sort of porch, provided with benches and uniformly of wood."
—JAMES FENIMORE COOPER, *The Towns of Manhattan* (1892)

The lasting legacy of the Dutch in America is a style that we call Dutch Colonial, although the style known today is a fabricated version conceived long after New Netherland was gone. When we imagine a Dutch Colonial house, we see a gambrel roof with flared eaves, dormer windows, walls of shingles, and windows framed by shutters with half-moon cutouts. This image is a synthesis of historic Dutch and English traditions reinterpreted during the early 20th-century Colonial Revival as a new suburban vernacular.

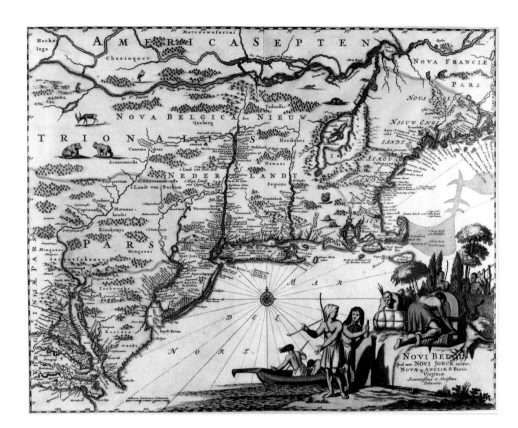

Built on the banks of the Connecticut River in the 1790s, the gambrel-roofed Benoni Stebbins House shows telltale signs of this Dutch-English heritage. The Stebbins House has been restored by architect Donald Rattner with additions that complement its original design. New gambrel roofs, clapboard walls, and Dutch doors add to the home's authentic pedigree and provide a window into the marriage of Dutch and English colonial building in the Hudson River Valley.

CHARTING THE HUDSON VALLEY

As English navigator Henry Hudson steered his ship, the *Halve Maen,* through the narrows between Staten Island and Long Island in the summer of 1609, he marveled at a virgin land of green plains and wooded hills at the mouth of a "Great River." Sailing for the merchants of Holland, Hudson searched in vain for the fabled Northwest Passage to the riches of Cathay and the Spice Islands of the Indies. He found instead a place that was destined to become a center of world commerce and create riches far beyond his imagination.

Hudson journeyed up the river that now bears his name while exploring the Atlantic coast of America for the Dutch Republic from 1607 to 1611. Although he failed to find a passage through the continent, his voyage turned out to be a triumph for the Dutch, for he had charted the Atlantic shoreline from Virginia to New England, laying claim to the territory of New Netherland.

The new Dutch colony spanned the coastline from the Delaware River to the Connecticut River. For years the Connecticut River remained a controversial but porous border with New England, where the two cultures met and exchanged traditions, especially in architecture. Among these traditions was the English gambrel roof that would become a Dutch icon.

In 1626, the Dutch West India Company founded a trading post on Manhattan Island when Director-General Peter Minuit bought the island from the Manhates Indians for 60 guilders, or roughly $24. From its founding, New Amsterdam was a cosmopolitan town, a bustling seaport, and a hub of international commerce.

New Netherland lasted only 40 years before King Charles II of England annexed the colony in 1664. The king gave the entire coastline from the Delaware to the Connecticut to his brother James, Duke of York, ignoring Dutch claims and renaming it New York. Faced with an armada of English warships gathered off New Amsterdam's shore, Dutch Director-General Peter Stuyvesant gave up the colony without a fight.

OLD-WORLD TRADITIONS IN NEW NETHERLAND

The colonists of New Netherland transplanted medieval building forms from Holland and Flanders to the Hudson River Valley. Traditions from the streets of Amsterdam, Leiden, and Utrecht filled the colonial towns of New Amsterdam (Manhattan) and Beverwyck (Albany).

Dutch colonial houses in the lower Hudson Valley, like the Guyon-Lake-Tysen house (1740) in Historic Richmond Town on Staten Island, were capped with shingles beneath a gambrel roof with strongly curved eaves. These features became the inspiration behind Dutch Colonial Revival houses in the early 20th century.

New Amsterdam (1702).

PIETER CLAESSEN WYCKOFF HOUSE

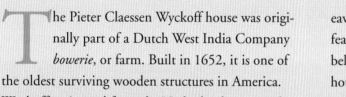

The Pieter Claessen Wyckoff house was originally part of a Dutch West India Company *bowerie*, or farm. Built in 1652, it is one of the oldest surviving wooden structures in America. Wyckoff emigrated from the Netherlands as an indentured servant in 1637 and purchased his farmstead from Peter Stuyvesant, then Director-General of New Netherland. Eventually, Wyckoff became the wealthiest citizen of the town of New Amersfoort, later called Canarsie or Flatbush.

The walls of the Wyckoff House are covered in hand-split shingles. Its distinctive Dutch Colonial flared eaves and anchor-bent timber frame are traditional features of the Long Island Dutch vernacular. What is believed to be the original 17th-century portion of the house, now the old kitchen, is a small wing with a low ceiling and a jambless Dutch fireplace.

The central hall of the 18th-century section was created when the roof was raised to enlarge the rear of the house. Open wall sections display the original timberframe construction, showing wooden studs filled with handmade bricks, insulated with mud and straw, and covered with plaster.

(far left) Once part of a Dutch farm called a bowerie, *the original portion of the Pieter Claessen Wyckoff House (1652) may be the oldest surviving wooden house in America.*

(left) Long hand-split shingles cover the walls of Wyckoff House, typical of Dutch Colonial homes on Long Island. The earliest part of the house includes a Dutch door of flat panels with a transom window above.

(opposite page) Within walls framed of anchor-bent timbers, the original 17th-century interior was modified in the 18th century to convert the house into a center-hall plan.

• anchor-bent •

The *anchor-bent* frame, a form of timber framing derived from German medieval barn construction, is typical of all Dutch Colonial building. The *anchor-bent* is a series of heavy H-shaped timber frames, spaced about 4 ft. apart along the length of the house, to which the exterior walls and floors are attached. The upper section of the H-frame provides usable loft space above the floor beams.

From the Dutch and Flemish lowlands came the building styles of western Long Island and the northern parts of New Jersey, each with its own distinctive character.

Since brick was the traditional building material of Holland, brick making began early in New York and Albany. As soon as a New Netherland merchant could afford one, he built a substantial brick townhouse in imitation of the houses of Amsterdam. In the Hudson Valley countryside, stone became the primary building material, especially among French Huguenots and Walloons, only because the much-preferred brick was too expensive to haul from the cities. Since there was little stone to be had on Long Island, houses there were built of wood-frame construction and sided in clapboards or hand-split shingles.

Whether a Dutch house was made of clapboards, shingles, brick, or stone, its distinctive architectural feature was a roof that projected out 2 ft. or more in front and back and was gracefully curved at the eaves. This Dutch Colonial "bell-cast" or "spring" eave, unsupported by columns, was probably of Flemish origin and was imported directly to the Dutch colony.

The typical Dutch Colonial house was only one room deep, with two or three rooms strung out in a long row, each with its own outside door split in half—the signature Dutch door. Before English Georgian floor plans became popular in the 1750s, Dutch houses seldom had center halls or interior hallways. They were built using a unique timber-framing technique called an anchor-bent frame, a common form that unites all Dutch Colonial architecture.

DUTCH COLONIAL ON THE CONNECTICUT

The banks of the Connecticut River may seem far afield for a Dutch Colonial house, but the Dutch considered the river they called the East River their boundary with New England. Facing the river, the late 18th-century Benoni Stebbins House, including architect Donald Rattner's recent renovations, revives the story of the Dutch presence in New England.

Built more than a century after the Dutch relinquished New Netherland, the original Stebbins House was not Dutch in plan. Instead, its layout was that of a classic 18th-century New England colonial built around a massive central chimney in a hall-and-parlor design. The front door faced the water, the main highway for

The new front entry foyer was part of the old Benoni Stebbins House, probably its original keeping room kitchen, with a brick cooking hearth and space for a built-in bake oven.

society and commerce in colonial times. The original house was covered with a gambrel roof and eaves that hinted at Dutch influences.

As often happened, though, over two centuries the Stebbins House was remodeled to become nearly unrecognizable. Rattner sorted through the hodge-podge of additions to create much-needed character revisions, taking his cue from the original gambrel roof and its shed dormers to recast the house as a modern-day Dutch Colonial Revival.

The house has been extended on both ends, just as the Dutch would have done, tripling its original size by adding a master bedroom suite, a new kitchen and dining room, and a family room. Using gambrel roofs for the new parts, Rattner has broken down the scale of the additions into smaller pieces, some of which are turned at right angles to the main house. The easygoing new old house has a unified, settled character that belies its size to appear small and comfortable.

To achieve this sense of comfort, the architect used a consistent palette of materials—white clapboard siding, wood shingle roofs, and trim shed dormers. Nothing new is jarring or out of scale with the early house but quietly fits in. Even the large double-hung windows on the new kitchen and bedroom wings, ganged together into groups of three, seem to blend in seamlessly.

The gambrel roof on the Stebbins House was used widely in colonial New England and northern New Jersey to add space to attic bedrooms. It precluded windows on the second floor, so dormers had to be added to open up bedrooms to sunlight. Traditional shed-roof dormers were made by extending the upper part of the house roof out over the dormers. In 1920s Dutch Colonial Revival houses, three or four dormer windows were often grouped together under one continuous shed roof, as Rattner has done for the long dormer above the dining room.

TELLING DETAIL

DUTCH FLARED EAVE

The classic Dutch roof and flared eave are probably Flemish in origin. In the maritime region of Flanders, now southern Holland, western Belgium, and the northern tip of France, farmhouses are found whose low walls are built of clay with flared eaves canti-levered out from the walls to protect the clay from washing away in the rain.

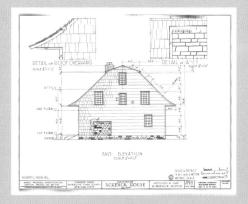

Dutch moments in a New England interior

While the front entry of the house has the obligatory Dutch door, the entrance door on the river side of the Stebbins House is not Dutch but English, a four-panel door hung on wrought-iron HL strap hinges. The door opens into a tiny New England vestibule rather than into a Dutch *kuchen* (living room, bedroom, and kitchen), as it would have in an early Dutch house. On the back wall of the vestibule is a classic, steep and narrow switch-back stair set against the central chimney and leading to upstairs bedrooms.

Vestiges of early colonial construction have been left visible in the new study and entry hall, formerly the original hall and hearth room of the 1790s house. In each room, heavy timber beams supporting smaller floor joists have been left exposed, as are the undersides of rough-sawn plank floorboards. The timbers are not part of a Dutch anchor-bent timber frame, however, but those of an English post-and-beam frame.

The newer rooms added to the Stebbins House are traditional but up-to-date, especially the generously proportioned kitchen. Ties to the older architecture are maintained in heavy trusses of rough-sawn wood that span the high ceiling. The ceiling rises up to the underside of its gambrel roof, shaping the room in an interior reminder of the external Dutch form.

In these subtle details the architect brings us back to the theme he has pursued throughout the renovation: recasting this late 18th-century landmark into a suggestion of how the Dutch Colonial style might have evolved over time.

By removing a welter of time-worn additions, Rattner recast the Stebbins House as a modern Dutch Colonial Revival, using new additions with a consistent palette of gambrel roofs and shed dormers.

THREE DUTCH TRADITIONS IN THE HUDSON VALLEY

Although the Dutch colony in the Hudson Valley was short-lived, its influences persisted for a century. New Netherland was the cradle for three strains of colonial architecture rather than one uniform style.

The farmhouses of New Netherland were distinctly different from the brick townhouses of New Amsterdam, not only because brick was largely unavailable in rural areas but also because Flemish building traditions were more influential there. Largely settled by Huguenot farmers, the towns of Ulster County in upstate New York are lined with stone houses that resemble the rural

DUTCH DOOR

The two-part Dutch door, split into two sections across the middle, was used on all early Dutch Colonial houses. The upper section could be opened for ventilation while the lower section was left closed to secure the house. The new front entrance added to the Stebbins House has a Dutch door that swings open into the entry hall.

farmhouses of Flanders, beneath steeply pitched roofs like those of Normandy.

Many Huguenot houses began as a single room and grew in length over time, with a large open fireplace on the north wall and a narrow corner stair leading to an attic and cellar. The attic was used to store grain, while the cellar kept meats and vegetables cool. The Bevier-Elting House (1698) in New Paltz, New York, was enlarged in three sections, its 2-ft.-thick stone walls joined together into one long linear house under a steep gable roof.

In Bergen County, New Jersey, an area on the Hudson first settled by Walloons, stone houses differed from those upriver. Here farmers built with red sandstone mortared together with burned oyster shell lime. The

The riverside doorway was the original front door to the Stebbins House, built at a time when the Connecticut River was the main thoroughfare for socializing and trade.

(above) Restored and enlarged by Donald Rattner, the original Benoni Stebbins House, built in the 1790s, is now the centerpiece for additions shaped by gambrel roofs and clapboard walls in the Dutch Colonial style.

(far left) White clapboard walls, natural cedar shingles, and unadorned window frames are the uniform repertoire of materials used throughout the house, making the new parts blend in seamlessly.

(left) The gambrel roof shape was shared by colonial New England and New Netherland, a design that created more headroom in attic bedrooms, with daylight and ventilation provided by dormer windows.

(opposite page) The up-to-date kitchen is framed by heavy wooden trusses that echo the timber framing of the original house.

Opening into a compact New England Colonial vestibule, the riverside door of the Stebbins House barely has room to swing in front of a steep and narrow switch-back stair that leads to second-floor bedrooms.

(left) The paneled study off the tiny entrance vestibule shows signs of its colonial past in an exposed ceiling of heavy timber beams that carry rough-sawn boards for the floor above.

Dutch homes on western Long Island, where stone was scarce, were built of wood frame with hand-split shingle walls. The shingled Jan Martense Schenck Farmhouse (1675) has the quintessentially Dutch Colonial gambrel roof and flared eaves.

(opposite page) Upstairs, the guest bedroom ceiling in the Stebbins House traces the shape of its gambrel roof, clearly showing how the gambrel form adds more headroom. Shed-dormer windows are cut into the lower part of the second-floor walls.

walls of the Samuel Desmarest House (1678) are chiseled sandstone blocks laid in regular courses. The work of quarrying, dressing, and laying such refined stonework was made possible by slave labor, encouraged by Dutch laws that offered settlers 75 acres of land for each slave.

On western Long Island, a land of open flats and tidal plains, stone was scarce but timber was plentiful. Carved into plantation farms, the countryside was dotted with one-and-a-half-story wooden farmhouses with walls sided in weatherboards or shingles. Long Island builders favored long hand-split shingles laid as much as 14 in. to the weather, their bottom edges rounded at the corners as a decorative detail.

Although not a farmer, Jan Martense Schenck built his house on Mill Island (present-day Flatbush) in 1675. Built next to a Dutch shipping channel, the house had a unique timber frame with curved timbers

The limestone walls of the Bevier-Elting House (1698) were harvested from nearby ledges where stone was easily quarried. Broken with sledgehammers, the rough stones were laid in irregular stacks set in clay mortar and limewashed for added weather protection.

In northern New Jersey, stone houses differed from those upriver because Flemish farmers built with red sandstone. The walls of the Samuel Desmarest House (1678) are chiseled sandstone blocks laid in lime mortar.

Dwight James Baum's 1920s designs for suburban homes, such as the Winchell House in the Riverdale, New York, neighborhood of Fieldston, show his inspired revival of the Dutch Colonial style.

resembling an upturned ship's hull. Its gambrel roof, flared eaves, and long hand-split-shingle walls represent the quintessential Dutch contribution to American house style, traditions that endured long after the colony's 40-year history ended.

DUTCH COLONIAL REVIVAL

Among Colonial Revival architects of the 1920s, Aymar Embury II (1880–1966) and Dwight James Baum (1886–1939) were the strongest proponents of the Dutch style. With thriving practices in the Hudson Valley, both men fashioned homes in an eclectic blend mixing early colonial traditions.

An architect as well as an architectural critic, Embury was the first to codify Dutch Colonial Revival design in his 1913 book *The Dutch Colonial House.* Baum lived and worked in the pastoral Riverdale section of New York City. His legacy endures in the planned community of Fieldston, where dozens of Dutch Colonial designs by Baum are still treasured today.

It is puzzling to find so little contemporary interest in the Dutch Colonial style, especially in the Hudson Valley where the style should be flourishing. While few new old houses are designed today in this picturesque, comfortable tradition, there is a clear opportunity for traditional architects to reinvent our Dutch heritage for the 21st century.

ABRAHAM HASBROUCK HOUSE

The original one-room Abraham Hasbrouck House, in the Huguenot Street Historic District of New Paltz, New York, was completed in 1692. As the Hasbrouck family grew, two additions were joined to the south gable end, enlarging the house under a continuous roof. With each extension, the floor level between interior rooms stepped down to follow the slope in grade.

The focal point of the interior is the center room, known as the "Room of Seven Doors." Its restored medieval fireplace is a jambless design that has no sidewalls, with a beehive chimney hood resting on heavy anchor-bent beams overhead. Fireplaces warmed most rooms of the house, but the bedroom was also heated by a Dutch stove made of cast-iron plates set low to the floor.

The Dutch *kas* in the center room dates from the 17th century, probably made in Holland and brought to New Netherland by one of the original settlers. Traditionally part of a woman's dowry, a kas was used as a wardrobe cabinet and also for storage of linens, needlework, silver, and pewter.

(far left) Heavy anchor-bent timber beams, spaced about 4 ft. apart, cross the ceiling above plastered stone walls. The early Dutch kas was used to store clothing and important family possessions.

(left) Built of rough ledgestone walls, the Abraham Hasbrouck House (1692) grew in length with two additions as new family members arrived, typical of the way Dutch Colonial houses in the Hudson Valley were enlarged.

PENNSYLVANIA DUTCH FARMHOUSE

"[Pennsylvania] is free for all Persuasions, in a Sober and Civil way; for the Church of England and the Quakers bear equal Share in the Government. They live Friendly and Well together; there is no Persecution for Religion, nor ever like to be."
—GABRIEL THOMAS, *An Account of West Jersey and Pennsylvania* (1698)

Daniel Boone was an American frontier legend who spent his childhood honing his wilderness skills in western Pennsylvania. The son of English Quaker parents, Boone was born in 1734 in a log and stone house in the Oley Valley near Reading. The Boones' neighbors were mostly Germans who had migrated to William Penn's colony to escape years of hardship and failing harvests in the Rhine River Valley. Although called Pennsylvania Dutch, they were not Dutch at all, but *Deutsch,* or Germans.

William Penn's Quaker colony, founded in 1682 on the Delaware River, attracted English Quakers and German Rhinelanders to the fertile farmland in the Schuylkill and Brandywine river valleys.

In the Pennsylvania Dutch country west of Philadelphia, architect Peter Zimmerman has re-created the classic story of a Quaker-German stone farmhouse. Starting with the strong bones of an 18th-century mill master's house, Zimmerman's new old house tells a tale of additions pieced together over 200 years. United by their common craftsmanship in stone, each part of his design records the subtle evolution of the Pennsylvania Dutch style, from German simplicity to Georgian grace.

WILLIAM PENN'S "HOLY EXPERIMENT"

The rolling hills and dales around Philadelphia, known as Pennsylvania Dutch country, are home to America's richest legacy of early stone farmhouses. At the turn of the 18th century, William Penn's "Holy Experiment"

attracted European peasants by the scores to his promise of religious freedom and fertile farmland in the Schuylkill and Brandywine river valleys. Out of the forests of the Pennsylvania countryside, English Quakers and German Rhinelanders cleared farmsteads and built houses of timber and stone, creating a distinctive Pennsylvania style.

Penn learned about building houses in the New World from Swedish log cabins built in the Delaware Valley and offered this advice to newcomers in a promotional pamphlet of 1684:

"…build then, a House of thirty foot long and eighteen foot broad, with a partition near the middle, and another to divide one end of the House into two small Rooms…with a loft over all….This may seem a mean way of Building but 'tis sufficient and safest for ordinary beginners."

Peter Zimmerman's new Pennsylvania Dutch stone farmhouse is set among the rolling hills on a Chester County farm that overlooks an old mill stream and a pond. Generations of additions have transformed the house from it's humble beginnings as a mill master's homestead.

(below) Made with fieldstones harvested from the nearby creek, the original mill master's house has a pent roof over the door and mortar joints made of coarse river sand and lime troweled flat. This was an ordinary mill building meant to be simple, sturdy, and unpretentious.

Penn's prescription became the "Quaker Plan" that guided early homebuilders in his colony. As they cleared fields and tilled the rock-strewn soils, Pennsylvania's Quaker and German settlers stockpiled logs and field-stones for building houses, barns, and outbuildings. Living together as neighbors, their cultures merged over time, weaving traditional English and German patterns of home into the classic Pennsylvania Dutch farmhouse.

All the building materials were close at hand, enabling settlers to shape homes that were truly of their place. The first log cabins built on Penn's plan lasted only for a generation before they were replaced by permanent houses of stone. Pennsylvania Germans pre-ferred to build in stone, as their ancestors had done, and they constructed a sturdier home as soon as they could.

Marriage of Quaker and German Traditions

Early Pennsylvania German stone houses often faithfully repeated the traditions of the Rhine Valley, where the common house was an *ernhaus,* also called a *flurküchenhaus,* arranged in three rooms built around a central chimney. In keeping with tradition, roofs were steeply pitched to provide sleeping room and storage in the attic.

Over time the ernhaus plan merged with the architecture of the English Quakers, and the classic Pennsylvania Dutch farmhouse was born. English colonial details such as a symmetrical facade, double-hung windows, and paneled wood shutters were combined with German floor plans and pent roofs. Two stories tall and square in plan, the classic house had three bays of windows across the front, an entry door offset to one side, and a chimney on the end wall.

With their farmsteads widely spaced across the countryside, Pennsylvania German families were independent and frugal. Architectural details were designed for utility rather than for show, and little attention was paid to decoration. The simple stone walls and lack of ornament bore witness to the values of simplicity and thrift that were shared by Quaker and German farmers.

(opposite page) In the 18th century, influenced by the Georgian style, the Pennsylvania Dutch farmhouse became more formal and symmetrical. This change in taste is shown in the Georgian portico and three-bay facade of the new house.

(far left) Pennsylvania Dutch stone walls were laid up in rough courses of fieldstone called rubblework. Heavy hewn oak beams were used to frame floors and roofs, while long hand-split oak shingles covered the roofs.

(left) The curved top and cross-buck bracing of Zimmerman's garden gate cast strong shadows in sunlight. A black iron ball-and-chain weight serves as the gate's latch.

HANS HERR HOUSE

Early German farmhouses were often built of fieldstone beneath a steep roof covered in hand-split oak shingles. The iconic example still standing is the restored Hans Herr House (1719) in Lancaster County. Herr was the patriarch of a group of Swiss Mennonites who followed an ancient Indian path, known as the Great Conestoga Road, to settle the western fringes of Pennsylvania.

The two-and-a-half-story Herr House is the earliest surviving stone house in Pennsylvania. Its fieldstone walls are buttered with mortar to make the rough stonework look smoothly finished.

Windows are irregularly placed in the walls, positioned by need rather than for symmetry, and protected by simple board-and-batten shutters.

The classic floor plan is built around a central chimney and divided into three first-floor rooms: a küche, a stube, and a kammer. The front door opens into the kitchen, with a narrow staircase in one corner that leads to second-floor bedchambers and an attic storage loft. The austere interiors reflect the stoicism of the German religious dissidents who first settled the Pennsylvania frontier.

(far left) Primitive interiors of roughcast plaster walls and wide plank floorboards recall the pragmatism and frugality of Pennsylvania's early German pioneers.

(left) A plank front door of molded boards fastened together with rose-head nails represents a single moment of artful detail in the making of this straightforward frontier home.

(opposite page) The restored Hans Herr House (1719) in Lancaster County is the oldest surviving example of an early Pennsylvania German farmhouse. Its walls are built of irregular fieldstones beneath a steep roof covered in hand-split oak shingles.

A Pennsylvania Dutch Story over Time

At the heart of Peter Zimmerman's reinvented Pennsylvania Dutch stone farmhouse is an 18th-century mill master's house that was once part of a grist mill. The mill, now vanished without a trace, stood on a nearby creek where the local farmers brought their grain to be milled into flour. The banks of the creek provided the limestone rock to build the original house and its mill.

Surrounded by an old barn and outbuildings, the new farmhouse joins imaginary period additions to the old mill master's house to re-create how the farmstead might have evolved over generations. The architect has made subtle distinctions between the parts, each detail describing a unique building period by the way the fieldstone is laid up in the walls, the degree of ornamentation on the doorways, and the style of dormer windows.

(left) The elaborate pediment and fluted pilaster columns of the portico surrounding the front door are late 18th-century Georgian in style.

(opposite page) The original fireplace in the mill master's house, now restored, is made of fieldstones surrounded by a mantel wall of beaded paneling, the simplest way to panel a wall in colonial times.

The front doorway and its elaborate classical door surround represent the late 18th-century Georgian style, while the original mill master's house has a less refined Dutch door that is early colonial. The small shed roof supported by angled brackets over the door to the garden wing is 20th-century Colonial Revival.

Variations in the stonework re-create distinct periods of stone building. The mill master's house is made of rough fieldstones harvested from the creek that are stacked in irregular courses called rubblework. By contrast, the stonework on the Georgian "addition" is more refined and better laid. The masons took more care to lay the fieldstones in courses, adding a tailored belt course, or raised band of stones, as a detail between the first and second floors.

Colonial dormers were an effective way to bring sunlight into upstairs attic bedrooms and storerooms. In their simplest form, they were designed as basic sheds

Designed to bring sunlight into upstairs rooms, dormers range from simple sheds to more refined gables, as seen on the garden wing where punched dormers poke through the eave line.

(opposite page) The new front door of six raised panels and fanlight window has achieved an aged patina by virtue of many coats of dark green-black paint applied in heavy brushstrokes. A graceful newel post, called a volute, and curved starter tread anchor the staircase.

to repel rain and snow. On the new old house, shed dormers appear over secondary wings, while prominent sections of the house such as the garden wing have fancier dormers typical of the 20th-century Colonial Revival. Their peaked roofs and crown moldings are more refined, cutting through the eaves in a style called a punched dormer.

Zimmerman's approach to re-creating a historic farmhouse owes a debt to Philadelphia architect R. Brognard Okie (1875–1945), an early 20th-century champion of Pennsylvania's unique architectural heritage. Okie's hand shows up in details large and small, as in Zimmerman's designs for fences, posts, and gates surrounding the house. A simple Okie-inspired post-and-rail fence sits on a stone wall leading to the front door. Rather than being mounted on top of the wall, the square posts are bolted into the stone face and gracefully tapered, turning a simple connection into a work of art.

Mimicking the patina of age

The stone walls and gate frame the front entrance to the new house. Designed like a classic 18th-century Georgian portico, the new front door looks hundreds of years old. Colonial builders turned to English pattern books for guidance in crafting such classical details. Here the six-panel door and fanlight window surrounded by pilaster columns and a pediment are brand new. The door has been painted a dozen times with dark green-black brushstrokes that imitate years of weathering to create a convincing patina of age.

The entry hall passes through the width of the house, past a gracious stair and its starter row of curved treads. Views from the stairhall into the living room are

(opposite page) In the dining room, Zimmerman designed the raised-panel wall surrounding the fireplace in early Pennsylvania Dutch style, with cupboard doors attached to their frames by reproduction wrought-iron H-hinges.

(far left) Deep arched doorways lined with raised panels frame views into the living room, where pairs of French doors open out to the garden terrace.

(left) While the formal focal point of the living room is its paneled mantelpiece, the real showstopper is the floor. With no carpet to cover them, the floorboards of rough-sawn wide oak planks are finished with layers of tung oil to a dark walnut color.

framed by two molded archways with keystones at their centers. The archways are lined with raised panels that make the walls appear thick, an effect the architect intended to mimic early interior partition walls that were often built of solid stone.

A Dutch door serves as the family entrance to the house, a traditional door style that was split in half to let fresh air in and keep farm animals out.

This new door has glass panes in the upper section and a bottom panel filled with beaded vertical planks. Classic 18th-century wrought-iron hardware attaches the new door to its frame.

The original main room of the mill master's house is now a sitting room, anchored by an old walk-in fireplace with a wrought-iron pot crane. The mantel wall is made of plain beaded planks painted colonial khaki green. This was the simplest form of colonial paneling to build, identifying this as the oldest part of the house.

At the far end of the house, a new guest bedroom looks as if it might have been the original bedchamber. Its masonry fireplace is coated inside and out with layers of white plaster, used in colonial times to protect stonework from the heat of the fire. The room has small windows with deep sills and rounded plaster jambs that re-create the typical frameless windows of a Pennsylvania Dutch farmhouse.

TESTAMENTS IN STONE

Pennsylvania Germans were scattered in a wide arc around the city of Philadelphia, settling in Bucks, Lancaster, York, and Chester counties, where they left behind a legacy of Pennsylvania Dutch farmhouses.

During the winter of 1777–78, generals George Washington and James Varnum camped out at Valley Forge to plan their spring campaigns, and both made their headquarters in stone farmhouses lent to the war effort. Varnum's headquarters, the David Stephens House (1750s), recalls German traditions in its steeply pitched roof, pent eaves, and small, irregular windows. By contrast, Washington's headquarters, the Isaac Potts House (1773), is more formal and symmetrical in the English Quaker style, with a shallower roof and evenly spaced double-hung windows set in a Georgian three-bay facade.

These traditional farmhouses are reflected in Zimmerman's new old house design. His Georgian facade shares the massing and formal symmetry of the Isaac Potts House, with three window bays and an offset front door. The attached wings, on the other hand, are more primitive in detail and modest in size, resembling the simpler David Stephens House. Added to these is a breezeway that looks like a plain farmhouse porch enclosed with walls of windows.

The farmhouse of David Stephens (1750s) at Valley Forge represents the early Pennsylvania German tradition of building with fieldstones laid as coarse rubblework, beneath a steeply pitched roof with pent eaves and small, irregularly spaced windows.

The Valley Forge house of Isaac Potts (1773) shows the evolution of Pennsylvania farmhouse design toward more formal Georgian symmetry, with evenly spaced double-hung windows set in a three-bay facade.

AFTER THE CENTENNIAL, BORN AGAIN

Time passed by the vernacular architecture of the Pennsylvania Dutch until the early 20th century, when architects and antiquarians of the Philadelphia School began to study their regional heritage. Like the Shingle Style revival in turn-of-the-century New England, the renaissance of Pennsylvania's Quaker-German architecture was stimulated by the Philadelphia Centennial Exhibition of 1876.

In the 1920s, architect Eleanor Raymond (1887–1989) was drawn to the simple vernacular structures of the Pennsylvania countryside, and in 1931 she published *Early Domestic Architecture of Pennsylvania*. The book was one of the first inventories of the state's vernacular traditions, documenting houses, barns, and outbuildings in photographs and measured drawings that showcase their "unstudied directness in fitting form to function."

Architect Okie wrote the foreword to Raymond's book, and he also became a master of the Pennsylvania Dutch vernacular. Practicing in Philadelphia, Okie devoted his career to restoring and re-creating "the old buildings [that] are beautifully proportioned, even the simplest woodshed or spring house." His credits include restorations of the Betsy Ross House and Penn's estate, Pennsbury Manor.

Like Okie, Zimmerman is a traditional architect dedicated to the preservation and rebirth of the architectural legacy of his native Pennsylvania. Part of a new generation of regional architects that includes John Milner and Archer & Buchanan, he is fostering a rebirth of the Pennsylvania Dutch style.

PEACEABLE FARM

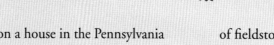

Coming upon a house in the Pennsylvania countryside by R. Brognard Okie is like finding long-buried treasure. Virtually unknown today to all but architecture buffs, Okie's signature style was an inventive blend of Pennsylvania farmhouse and English Cotswold cottage brought to life in rugged fieldstone and white clapboard siding. From the 1910s through the 1940s, Okie restored and added on to many of the forgotten farmsteads in Philadelphia's outer counties to create picturesque country houses.

Sitting in the rolling fields of Bucks County, Peaceable Farm is an Okie gem that has been meticulously restored. Designed in the 1930s as a dairy farm, the house and farm complex includes a barn, stables, blacksmith's shop, and stone cottage built around a working farmyard.

Peaceable Farm is a classic Pennsylvania Quaker-German stone farmhouse with an attached wing of white clapboards. The walls are rough, irregular blocks of fieldstone laid in a random pattern, with larger cornerstones reinforcing the wall corners. Second-floor windows pop up through the roof in punched dormers inspired by English cottages.

The roof eave is a plain square box that encloses the gutters, with more gutter boxes mounted below the windows to collect downspout water—a classic Okie detail. A traditional Pennsylvania Dutch door hood covers the front door, always built without supporting posts.

A shallow sitting porch framed in clapboard siding is carved into the wing of the house. From here, a doorway opens into the dining room and its large plastered fireplace set in paneled walls. Natural woodwork throughout the interior is stained a deep caramel color, while wide oak floorboards are fastened in place by wrought-iron nails. Every door in the house is hung on iron HL hinges re-created from early Pennsylvania prototypes.

(above left) R. Brognard Okie's Peaceable Farm was inspired by early Pennsylvania Dutch homes, its walls made of coarse fieldstone laid in an irregular pattern. Okie's trademark punched dormers project through the eave line, while his signature gutter boxes run below the windows.

(above right) The back entrance hall winds through a suite of doors from a primitive board-and-buck to a refined sash-and-panel, united by traditional Pennsylvania Dutch wrought-iron latch pulls, box locks, and strap hinges.

(left) The dining room and its plaster-lined fireplace are surrounded by mellow walls of caramel-colored woodwork and wide oak floorboards face-nailed in place.

TEXAS GERMAN HILL COUNTRY RANCH

"The German emigrants who came to the hill country of South-Central Texas . . . gave the land an identifying mark by erecting structures that combine traditional German influences . . . in houses and service buildings constructed of half-timbering or rock-and-mortar methods . . . [and] seemingly endless rock fences [of] local limestone."
—HUBERT WILHELM, *Organized German Settlement and Its Effects on the Frontier of South-Central Texas* (1968)

The gentle hills and valleys that rise northwest of San Antonio are home to a unique Texas subculture known as the Hill Country. The landscape is laced with small towns and ranches that border the Medina, Guadalupe, and Pedernales rivers. This was Indian Territory in Spanish Texas before scores of European immigrants came to settle here in the 1830s. Now there is a distinctive German flavor to the Texas Hill Country preserved in foothills settled by Hessian, Saxon, Rhineland, and Alsatian pioneers in the early 19th century.

Designed by Ignacio Salas-Humara
on a hill overlooking the Medina
River, Misty Hills Ranch commands
views of one of the Hill Country's
majestic valleys where European
immigrants first settled in Texas.

(opposite page) Built of soft yellow
Texas limestone, the mid 19th-century
Alfred Henke House near Fredericksburg showcases the fine masonry skills
of German pioneers who built Texas
rock houses in the Hill Country.

In the heart of the Medina Valley, a new ranch called Misty Hills commands a hilltop site overlooking river bottomland. Designed by architect Ignacio Salas-Humara, the house is a catalog of Hill Country traditions recalling the history of Texas German architecture—a ranch house, wagon barn, bunkhouse, and water tower knit together into a rambling residence. The new old house captures the region's country roots shaped in mellow Texas limestone, vintage timbers, and rusted metal roofs.

SETTLING TEXAS

The Mexican War of Independence (1810–21) spelled the beginning of the end of Spanish influence in Texas, closed forever by the Texas Revolution of 1836. Sam Houston, president of the newly minted Republic of Texas, sent out a call to Europe and America for settlers to come populate his new republic, luring them to the

frontier with generous grants of land. Driven from their farms by bitter cold winters, failing crops, and exorbitant prices in 1830s Europe, German pioneers heeded the call and came to make a fresh start in Texas.

They came from Hesse, the Rhineland, and Lower Saxony in Germany, as well as from Alsace in France. The verdant hills west of San Antonio beckoned with wide open meadows, live oaks and cedars, limestone soils, and abundant water. Peasant farmers soon imprinted the landscape of the Hill Country with a unique personality colored by German and Alsatian traditions in towns such as New Braunfels, Castroville, Comfort, and Fredericksburg.

In the 1840s, the *Adelsverein,* a German benevolent society, set out to build a "New Fatherland" in Texas. From the ports of Galveston and Matagorda, German

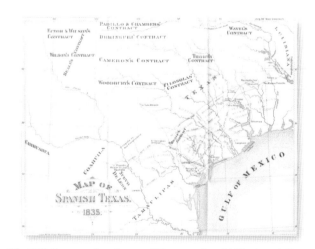

The Hill Country of south-central Texas was Spanish Territory before it was settled by German Rhinelanders, French Alsatians, and Appalachian highlanders in the 1830s.

immigrants headed inland toward San Antonio and its promising farmland. Their first colony was founded at New Braunfels in 1845, followed a year later by Fredericksburg, and eventually by a chain of settlements in the "German Belt" stretching from San Antonio to Mason. The area also attracted Frenchman Henri Castro, an early settler in the Medina Valley, who founded the town of Castroville and cultivated a distinctly Alsatian architecture in his "Little Alsace."

Waves of Anglo-Americans had preceded the Germans to the Hill Country, mostly southern mountaineers from the Ozarks and Appalachians of Kentucky, Tennessee, and Arkansas who flooded into the countryside around Austin. Founded in 1823 by Stephen Austin, the colony of San Felipe de Austin became home to English and Scots-Irish settlers who were entrepreneurs as well as farmers.

From the Appalachian highlands, these Anglo-Americans brought their heritage of building single-

pen and dogtrot log cabins. As they cleared fields of the weed tree of Texas, the cedar, they also began one of the state's earliest industries—the manufacture of cedar roof shingles—earning the nickname "cedar choppers" in the bargain.

Their new German neighbors soon picked up on the advantages of building with logs. But the industrious

Sheltered beneath a canopy of mature live oaks, the Carl Wilhelm Rummel House (1870) is a classic 19th-century Texas rock house that merges the stone-building traditions of German pioneers with Anglo-American influences such as the recessed front porch and second-floor dormers.

Appalachian highlanders brought pioneer log building to Stephen Austin's colony as early as 1823. As they cleared fields, the Anglo-Americans built single-pen and dogtrot log cabins, such as these restored cabins at the Lyndon Baines Johnson Ranch in GillespieCounty.

(opposite page) Built of many pieces of salvaged history, Misty Hills Ranch incorporates antique building materials such as old beams and weathered metal roofs, as well as reconstructed buildings such as a dogtrot log cabin used as a bedroom wing.

Germans craved more permanent homes, and at the first flush of prosperity, they replaced logs with stone. With every hillside ledge offering soft and easily workable Texas limestone, German craftsmen revived old-world masonry traditions honed in the Rhine River Valley to build farmhouses of cut stone, creating what became known as a Texas "rock house." Plentiful stands of live oaks furnished timbers for framing porches, floors, and roofs.

HOUSE OF SALVAGED PARTS

Ignacio Salas-Humara's Misty Hills Ranch is a new Texas rock house designed as a field guide to the history of Hill Country architecture. Drawing inspiration from the region's German, Alsatian, and American pasts, Salas-Humara conceived the house as a collection of historic artifacts strung together into a new old house. Some of the parts are salvaged buildings, such as a 19th-century dogtrot log cabin, while others are authentic re-creations built of old materials—antique beams, reclaimed stone, and weathered metal roofs.

Misty Hills Ranch basks in Lone Star style. The centerpiece is a pumped-up version of a Hill Country "Sunday House," a diminutive historic weekend home typical of Castroville and Fredericksburg. Here the Sunday House is all grown up in a full-size ranch house built of 18-in.-thick limestone walls and old hand-hewn oak beams.

Misty Hill's rock walls and weathered timbers were gathered from old and dilapidated barns. Many of the oak lintel beams used over windows and doors have notches and wooden pegs left over from original mortise-and-tenon joinery. The long porch stretching across the front wall is made of paired oak posts and timber rafters that are covered by a roof of rusty

TEXAS SUNDAY HOUSE

⌁

Built by Hill Country Germans as in-town weekend retreats, Sunday Houses or Sabbath Houses were places where they could attend church, go shopping, and socialize with neighbors while taking a break from their ranches in the outback. Early Sunday Houses were built of German *fachwerk* half-timbering or limestone rock, with one large room warmed by a fireplace and a sleeping loft above reached by an outside stair. There was almost always a porch across the front to welcome visitors.

(above left) The hand-hewn posts, beams, and rafters of the front porch were salvaged from dilapidated barns. They support an old corrugated steel roof that adds antiqued charm to the house.

(above right) Timeworn oak beams on a porch of antique timbers and embedded in the stonework serve as lintels over windows and doors, still showing telltale marks of being hewn with a broadax.

(left) Stretched across the front of the new Sunday House, the front porch is made of antique timber posts and rafters with ax marks, notches, and pegs left over from old timber framing.

corrugated metal panels. The roof may look as if it came from the junk pile, but such timeworn sheet metal is prized like a rare antique and priced to match.

Tied in to the main house like a feline tail is the bedroom wing for the children, a reconstructed dog-trot log cabin reassembled by Salas-Humara. Texas log cabins were distinct from the tightly-fit-together cabins of the Appalachian frontier. The wide spaces left over between cross-stacked logs were filled with stones and

mortar, creating a chinking pattern that is distinct in the Hill Country.

At the far end of the log cabin, more building parts are attached. First, there is a short corridor made of weathered board-and-batten siding that runs into what looks like the head house of a mine shaft. This in turn is connected to a two-story garage resembling an old western bunkhouse and stone wagon barn. The fortress-like garage doors are made of heavy wooden planks hung on forged-iron strap hinges.

As big as Texas

Misty Hills' solid stone walls make the house appear dark from the outside, but inside it is a cool retreat bathed in sunlight. The exposed limestone interior walls are a thick insulating layer of stone that stays cool despite the searing Texas heat. Everything on the inside is overscaled, with ceilings of gnarled beams and rough-sawn boards that tower 14 ft. overhead. There are pairs of windows on every outside wall that are taller than a man, combined with glass-and-panel doors that wick light into the interior.

None of this bigness is particularly historic, for original Sunday Houses had but a few small windows and a couple of solid plank doors. They were tiny in size, designed to be compact in every dimension. Here the dramatic change in scale completely alters the experience from cozy to commanding.

A fireplace the size of an old cooking hearth is the centerpiece of this Texas version of a keeping room, fitted out with a forged-iron pot crane and a distressed mantelpiece to shelve pewterware.

(above) Similar to the Gerhard Ihnken House (1851) in Castroville (above right), the garage is two stories tall with a bunkhouse for guest rooms on the second floor. The rugged garage doors are thick wooden planks reinforced by cross bucks and mounted on wrought-iron strap hinges.

(right) Despite the house's thick stone walls, the interior is bathed in sunlight drawn through oversized windows matching the exaggerated scale of the new Sunday House. Walls of stone keep the interior cool in the Texas heat.

Adding a convincing patina of age to the house, pairs of French doors have been custom made in rough-sawn wood. The doors latch with rusted lever handles mounted on scrolled back plates.

Vintage roots

The kitchen, breakfast room, and family sitting room fill one large space arranged around a central hearth. Salas-Humara got the idea for connected living spaces from the keeping room of a New England Colonial house, where the family cooked its meals, did domestic chores, and socialized around the warmth of a fire. Here, the kitchen is a 21st-century version of the keeping room done Texas size.

The dogtrot log cabin shows up in the interior as a hallway for the children's bedrooms. Each bedroom has walls of exposed logs that are nearly two stories tall, the full height of the original cabin, and high enough to accommodate a loft space above. Getting up close to the log walls, one can study their timeworn texture and the stone-and-lime mortar used to chink them.

Every piece of antique building material incorporated into the house lends authenticity to its story. Old timbers shaped by broadax become lintels over doorways; rough-sawn planks cover the floors; and iron wagon-wheel chandeliers light up the entrance hall. Most intriguing are the glass-and-panel doors assembled from weather-beaten wood that come with ragged faces etched by time. Adding character are vintage hinges and wrought-iron locksets with scalloped back plates and curved palm latches burnished by years of use.

There is one last vintage surprise to delight the eye: a wooden barrel-stave water tank that seems out of place sitting atop a stone wing of the house. Water towers covered by corrugated metal roofs were a common sight on Texas Hill Country ranches, mounted high in the air on a stone base to generate water pressure. Built in Australia, the new water tank is a bit of re-created Texas history designed to be part of the working water system. Such antique reminders seeded into every corner of Misty Hills Ranch leave no doubt that this is a new house with deep roots in Texas's past.

TEXAS ROCK HOUSES

The Texas Hill Country was a latecomer to America's architectural story, taking shape only after Stephen Austin and Sam Houston had left their mark on the former Spanish borderlands in the 1830s. Freed from Spain and then Mexico, the future of the Texas Republic was fortified by the resolve of its European immigrants. They built stalwart Texas rock houses meant to last on farmsteads across the hills and valleys.

Examples of well-preserved houses abound across the Texas Hill Country where German craftsmen re-created old-world building traditions, learning a thing or two from their American neighbors along the way. First they tried fachwerk, a form of German timber framing where a skeleton of timber posts and beams formed the structural frame. Open wall spaces were filled in with adobe bricks or stones and covered with layers of whitewash or weatherboards.

As German building traditions matured during the 19th century, they bent toward American style. Built without a timber frame, the Rudolph Von Schorobiny House (1850s) in the Alsatian community of Quihi is an early Texas rock house of solid limestone. Its front porch is an American model adapted by the Germans who learned the value of a sheltering porch in the sun-baked climate.

They even tried the saltbox shape, a familiar form from colonial homes in New England. The barn of the John Peter Tatsch House (1852) in Fredericksburg is a saltbox type made of vertical boards over a timber frame with wooden battens covering the butt joints between boards.

Still later, house forms began to resemble the American Federal and Greek Revival styles, featuring two-story gables and symmetrical patterns for windows and doors. German and American traditions blended seamlessly into a new Texas style. The 1870 Carl Wilhelm Rummel House in Round Top (see the left photo on p. 250) shows an American form grafted onto a Texas rock house with a classic front porch and supporting columns. The Johann Traugott Wantke House (1863) looks like a distant cousin of a Pennsylvania Dutch farmhouse covered by a steep roof with a sturdy stone chimney.

The new barrel-stave water tank sitting on top of a stone base re-creates another piece of Texas Hill Country history, where water towers covered by corrugated metal roofs were a ranch fixture.

(opposite page) The kitchen of Misty Hills Ranch is built into one end of a large room where a stone hearth surrounds the commercial range. As in the rest of the house, the ceiling towers 14 ft. overhead.

Built of limestone in the Alsatian town of Quihi, the Rudolph Von Schorobiny House (1850s) is an early rock house that shares a front porch similar to those on German Sunday Houses.

SUNDAY HOUSE REVIVAL

As is true of many American vernacular traditions, early Texas folk architecture has been overlooked for generations. Only recently have architects considered reviving Texas traditions, especially the Texas Hill Country style. Today's architects have begun to take a fresh look at this tradition, motivated in no small part by clients captivated by the small Sunday Houses of Castroville and Fredericksburg.

Architect Stephen Chambers has re-created an early German Sunday House as the guest cottage for Fulton Ranch in Wise County. The new cottage is a study in Sunday House architecture, its stone walls, attached front porch, and broken saltbox roofline inspired by the best historic examples.

Chambers's cottage is made of limestone rocks that have been dressed and squared more precisely than on early rock houses, with arched stone headers over traditional casement windows typical of Alsatian-style houses. The standing-seam metal roof has the tall pitch and tapered saltbox shape of a historic Sunday House, with a raised front porch that stretches across the front. A modern interpretation of classic Hill Country style, Chambers's design show-cases the simple, enduring beauty of 19th-century Texas German architecture.

The saltbox form of the John Peter Tatsch Barn (1852), built of vertical board-and-batten siding, shows how the New England saltbox shape found a home in Texas.

Resembling a Pennsylvania Dutch stone farmhouse, the Johann Traugott Wantke House (1863) in Round Top shares the steep roof and sturdy chimney commonly inherited from the German Rhineland.

(left) Architect Stephen Chambers's guesthouse at Fulton Ranch in Wise County re-creates a Sunday House in a new limestone cottage with the familiar front porch and broken saltbox roofline of historic originals.

(above left) A sitting porch stretches across the front of the new guesthouse—classic feature of Texas Sunday houses designed as shelter from the sun and a gathering place to socialize with neighbors.

(above right) A screened-in porch is a private outdoor room tucked under the saltbox roof at the back of the house.

ALFRED HENKE HOUSE

Although built near the German Hill Country town of Fredericksburg, the mid 19th-century Alfred Henke House is much closer in character to the Alsatian homes of Castroville. Alsace was a disputed region in the western Rhine Valley that straddled France and Germany, its Catholic farmers having stronger French ties than their German Protestant neighbors. Despite being separated by religious beliefs, both Rhineland cultures shared the common tradition of building in stone.

The two-story Henke House shows the subtle character of Alsatian building in walls made of limestone rocks that have been carefully stacked. The stone corners are interlocked with alternating larger blocks called quoins. Stone relieving arches over the windows and doors support the weight of the wall above. The few windows on the facade are symmetrically arranged and deeply recessed into the stonework. Covered by a shallow roof of standing-seam metal, the house has a chimney at each gable end.

Unlike classic German Sunday Houses, which had one large room and an outside stair to the attic, the Henke House is a center-hall plan with two parlors and a formal interior stair to the second floor. Instead of a saltbox extension across the back, there is a two-story dining room and bedroom wing under a gable roof. While most Alsatian houses had a front porch set on the ground over paving stones, the Henke House may never have had a porch. It is likely that the walls were originally plastered or painted with limewash as was common in Little Alsace.

Two bedrooms and one large bunkroom share the second-floor loft at the top of the stairs beneath a ceiling of rough-sawn timbers.

(far left) A stone relieving arch made of limestone blocks carries the weight of the wall over the front door, framed by a transom window and sidelights.

(left) The restored kitchen wing of exposed stone walls and timber ceiling takes on the casual character of French Provence.

(below) The austere stone walls of the Alfred Henke House, built of soft yellow Texas limestone carefully stacked in rough courses, share the sober Alsatian character of the homes of Castroville.

PHOTO CREDITS

p. 9: (top) Photo courtesy National Register of Historic Places Photographic Files, South Carolina Department of Archives and History

OUR SPANISH HERITAGE

p. 20: Map courtesy Birmingham Public Library, Agee Map Collection, Birmingham, Alabama

p. 21: (center) Photo courtesy Library of Congress, Prints and Photographs Division, Historic American Buildings Survey

p. 22: Map courtesy Birmingham Public Library, Agee Map Collection, Birmingham, Alabama

p. 24: Map courtcsy Thomason Room of the Newton Gresham Library, Sam Houston State University, Huntsville, TX

p. 29: (top) Map courtesy Birmingham Public Library, Agee Map Collection, Birmingham, Alabama; (bottom left) Photo reprinted with permission of the University Press of Florida; (bottom right) Photo courtesy Library of Congress, Prints and Photographs Division, Historic American Buildings Survey

p. 36: (right) Photo courtesy Library of Congress, Prints and Photographs Division, Historic American Buildings Survey

p. 37: Photos courtesy Library of Congress, Prints and Photographs Division, Historic American Buildings Survey

p. 39: (top) Photo courtesy Duany Plater-Zyberk & Co.; photographer: Carlos I. Morales/Carpe Luz

p. 44: (top) Map courtesy Virginia Garrett Cartographic History Library, Special Collections, The University of Texas at Arlington Library, Arlington, Texas; (bottom) Photo courtesy Library of Congress, Prints and Photographs Division, Historic American Buildings Survey

p. 46: Photo by Russell Versaci

p. 50: Photo courtesy Library of Congress, Prints and Photographs Division, Historic American Buildings Survey

p. 54: Photos courtesy Library of Congress, Prints and Photographs Division, Historic American Buildings Survey

p. 55: (bottom left and top) Photos courtesy Library of Congress, Prints and Photographs Division, Historic American Buildings Survey

p. 56: (top left) Photo courtesy *The Old Mission Churches and Historic Houses of California* by Robert Newcomb, © 1925 J.B. Lippincott Company; (top right and middle right) Photos courtesy Library of Congress, Prints and Photographs Division, Historic American Buildings Survey; (bottom right) Photo Wikipedia

p. 60: (top right) Map courtesy of the Library of Congress; (bottom right) Photo courtesy Library of Congress, Prints and Photographs Division, Historic American Buildings Survey

p. 61: (top) Drawing courtesy *The Old Mission Churches and Historic Houses of California* by Robert Newcomb, © 1925 J.B. Lippincott Company; (bottom) Photo courtesy Library of Congress, Prints and Photographs Division, Historic American Buildings Survey

p. 69: (bottom left and top) Photos courtesy Library of Congress, Prints and Photographs Division, Historic American Buildings Survey

pp. 70–71: Photos courtesy Library of Congress, Prints and Photographs Division, Historic American Buildings Survey

p. 72: Photo courtesy *Western Ranch Houses,* by Cliff May, published by Hennessey + Ingalls, Santa Monica, CA

OUR FRENCH HERITAGE

p. 76: Map courtesy of the Library of Congress

p. 77 (bottom left) Photo by Douglas Bock; (middle) Photo courtesy Library of Congress, Prints and Photographs Division, Historic American Buildings Survey

p. 78: Photo courtesy Library of Congress, Prints and Photographs Division, Historic American Buildings Survey

p. 79: *French North America to the middle of the eighteenth century* by Van H. English, reproduced in *Early American Architecture: From the Colonial Settlements to the National Period* by Hugh Morrison, Oxford University Press, Inc., 1952

p. 80: (left) Drawing courtesy *Small French Buildings,* plate 32, by Lewis A. Coffin, et. al., Charles Scribner's Sons, 1926; (right) Drawing courtesy Missouri Historical Society, St. Louis

p. 85: (left) Map courtesy of the Library of Congress; (right) Photo courtesy Library of Congress, Prints and Photographs Division, Historic American Buildings Survey

p. 86: (right) Collot, Georges Henri Victor, *French Habitation in the Country of the Illinois.* Yale Collection of Western Americana, Beinecke Rare Book and Manuscript Library, Yale University.

p. 92: Drawing courtesy Library of Congress, Prints and Photographs Division, Historic American Buildings Survey

p. 94: (left) Photo courtesy Library of Congress, Prints and Photographs Division, Historic American Buildings Survey; (right) Photo by Philip Gould

p. 100: (top) Map courtesy I.N. Phelps Stokes Collection, Miriam and Ira D. Wallach Division of Art, Prints and Photographs, The New York Public Library, Astor, Lenox and Tilden Foundations; (bottom right) Drawing courtesy of the Library of Congress

p. 101: (left) Photo courtesy Louisiana State Museum; (right) Drawing courtesy Library of Congress, Prints and Photographs Division, Historic American Buildings Survey

p. 106: Photo courtesy Library of Congress, Prints and Photographs Division, Historic American Buildings Survey

p. 109 (left) Photo courtesy Louisiana State Museum; (right) Photo courtesy Library of Congress, Prints and Photographs Division, Historic American Buildings Survey

p. 110: Drawing courtesy Library of Congress, Prints and Photographs Division, Historic American Buildings Survey

p. 111: (top right) Photo provided by Koch and Wilson Architects; (bottom right) Photo by Douglas Bock

OUR ENGLISH HERITAGE

p. 114: Map courtesy Birmingham Public Library, Agee Map Collection, Birmingham, Alabama

p. 115: (center) Photo courtesy Library of Congress, Prints and Photographs Division, Historic American Buildings Survey

p. 118: Map courtesy Birmingham Public Library, Agee Map Collection, Birmingham, Alabama

p. 119: (left) Photo reproduced with permission from English Heritage NMR; (right) Drawing courtesy Special Collections, University of Virginia Library

p. 123: Map courtesy Collection of the Maryland State Archives Special Collections (Huntingfield Map Collection) John Ogilby, *Noua Terrae-Mariae Tabula*, 1671, MSA SC 1399-1-187

p. 126: (bottom left) Photo courtesy Library of Congress, Prints and Photographs Division, Historic American Buildings Survey

p. 131: (bottom right) Photo by Bill Snead

p. 134: (bottom right) Photo courtesy Library of Congress, Prints and Photographs Division, Historic American Buildings Survey

pp. 135–137: Photos courtesy Library of Congress, Prints and Photographs Division, Historic American Buildings Survey

p. 140: (bottom) Photo courtesy G.E. Kidder Smith, Courtesy of Kidder Smith Collection, Rotch Visual Collections, M.I.T.

p. 141: (top) *New England settlements about 1650* by Van H. English, reproduced in *Early American Architecture: From the Colonial Settlements to the National Period* by Hugh Morrison, Oxford University Press, Inc., 1952; (bottom) Photo reproduced with permission from English Heritage NMR

p. 142: Drawings courtesy *Early Domestic Architecture of Connecticut* by J. Frederick Kelly, © 1924 Yale University Press

p. 149: (bottom left) Photo courtesy Library of Congress, Prints and Photographs Division, Historic American Buildings Survey

p. 150: Photo courtesy Royal Barry Wills Associates, Richard Wills

p. 151: (top) Photo courtesy Sears; (bottom) Photos courtesy Library of Congress, Prints and Photographs Division, Historic American Buildings Survey

p. 153: (left) Photo by Russell Versaci

p. 156: (top) Map courtesy Birmingham Public Library, Agee Map Collection, Birmingham, Alabama; (bottom) Photo courtesy of the National Library of Jamaica

p. 158: (top) Photo courtesy Library of Congress, Prints and Photographs Division, Historic American Buildings Survey

p. 165: (top) Photo courtesy Library of Congress, Prints and Photographs Division, Historic American Buildings Survey; (bottom) Photo courtesy South Carolina Dept. of Archives and History

p. 166 (right) Photo by Van Jones Martin

p. 172: Map courtesy Birmingham Public Library, Agee Map Collection, Birmingham, Alabama

p. 173: (bottom left) Photo courtesy Library of Congress, Prints and Photographs Division, Historic American Buildings Survey

p. 174: Photos courtesy Library of Congress, Prints and Photographs Division, Historic American Buildings Survey

p. 182: (top) Map from *The Early Architecture of Charleston*, courtesy of The University of South Carolina Press; (bottom) Photos courtesy Library of Congress, Prints and Photographs Division, Historic American Buildings Survey

p. 184: (bottom left) Photo courtesy Library of Congress, Prints and Photographs Division, Historic American Buildings Survey; (bottom right) Photo courtesy Angela Seckinger

OUR CONTINENTAL HERITAGE

p. 186: Map courtesy David Rumsey Map Collection, www.davidrumsey.com

p. 187: (left) Photo by Durston Saylor; (middle) Photo courtesy Library of Congress, Prints and Photographs Division, Historic American Buildings Survey

p. 189: (left) Drawing courtesy Court Street, Albany, NY, Pen & Ink, L. F. Tantillo; (right) Drawing courtesy Collection of The New York Historical Society

p. 190: (top) Courtesy Sears

p. 191: Photo courtesy Library of Congress, Prints and Photographs Division, Historic American Buildings Survey

p. 196: Map courtesy mapsofpa.com

p. 197: (bottom left) Drawing courtesy Collot, Georges Henri Victor, *An American Log-House*, Yale Collection of Western Americana, Beinecket Rare Book and Manuscript Library, Yale University

p. 198: (top left) Photo courtesy Archives and Special Collections, Berea College; (bottom left) Photo courtesy Library of Congress, Prints and Photographs Division, Historic American Buildings Survey

p. 199: (bottom left) Photo courtesy Lewes Historical Society, Lewes, DE; (bottom right) Photo courtesy Library of Congress, Prints and Photographs Division, Historic American Buildings Survey

p. 206: (top) Photo courtesy Archives and Special Collections, Berea College; (bottom) Photos courtesy Library of Congress, Prints and Photographs Division, Historic American Buildings Survey

p. 207: (left) Photo by Steve Speer; (right) Photo courtesy Richard Weisser and SmokyPhotos.com

p. 208: Photo by Durston Saylor

p. 210: Map courtesy Bert Twaalfhoven Collection, Fordham University Library, Bronx, New York

p. 211: Drawing courtesy Bert Twaalfhoven Collection, Fordham University Library, Bronx, New York

p. 216: Drawing courtesy Library of Congress, Prints and Photographs Division, Historic American Buildings Survey

p. 219: (top) Photo by Durston Saylor

p. 222: (top) Photo by James A. Robertson, www.pbase.com/jimrob; (bottom) Photos courtesy Library of Congress, Prints and Photographs Division, Historic American Buildings Survey

p. 224: Photo courtesy Dwight James Baum Papers, Special Collections Research Center, Syracuse University Library

p. 228: Drawing courtesy Print Collection, Miriam and Ira D. Wallach Division of Art, Prints and Photographs, The New York Public Library, Astor, Lenox and Tilden Foundations

p. 231: (bottom left) Photo by Geoffrey Gross

p. 236: (bottom left) Photo courtesy Library of Congress, Prints and Photographs Division, Historic American Buildings Survey

p. 241: (bottom) Photos courtesy Library of Congress, Prints and Photographs Division, Historic American Buildings Survey

p. 248: (bottom) Map courtesy TXGenWeb

p. 250: (bottom left) Photo courtesy Library of Congress, Prints and Photographs Division, Historic American Buildings Survey; (bottom right) Photo by Russell Versaci

p. 256: (top right) Photo courtesy Library of Congress, Prints and Photographs Division, Historic American Buildings Survey

p. 260: Photos courtesy Library of Congress, Prints and Photographs Division, Historic American Buildings Survey

DIRECTORY OF ARCHITECTS

Our Spanish Heritage

(p. 26) **Jason Dunham**
Cooper Johnson Smith Architects
102 South 12th Street
Tampa, FL 33602
(813) 273-0034
www.cjsarch.com

(p. 42) **Michael G. Imber**
Michael G. Imber Architects
111 West El Prado
San Antonio, TX 78212
(210) 824-7703
www.michaelgimber.com

(p. 58) **Steven Giannetti**
Giannetti Architects & Interiors, Inc.
11740 San Vicente Blvd., Ste 204
Los Angeles, CA 90049
(310) 820-1329
www.giannettiarchitects.com

Our English Heritage

(p. 120) **Stephen Muse**
Muse Architects
7401 Wisconsin Avenue, Suite 500
Bethesda, MD 20814
(301) 718-8118
www.musearchitects.com

(p. 138) **Edward Sunderland (Design/Builder)**
Sunderland Period Homes
P. O. Box 362
East Windsor Hill, CT 06208
(860) 528-6608
www.sunderlandperiodhomes.com

(p. 154) **Jim Strickland, David Bryant**
Historical Concepts
430 Prime Point, Suite 103
Peachtree City, GA 30269
(770) 487-8041
www.historicalconcepts.com

(p. 170) **Donald Rattner**
Studio for Civil Architecture
462 Broadway, 3rd floor
New York, NY 10013
(212) 625-3336
www.thecivilstudio.com

Our French Heritage

(p. 82) **Ron Arnoult (Design/Builder)**
P. O. Box 185
206 Morgan St.
Madisonville, LA 70447
(985) 630-5653

(p. 98) **Mark Finlay**
Mark P. Finlay Architects
96 Old Post Road, Suite 200
Southport, CT 06890
(203) 254-2388
www.markfinlay.com

Our Continental Heritage

(p. 194) **Candace Tillotson-Miller**
Candace Tillotson-Miller Architects
P. O. Box 470
208 West Park Street
Livingston, MT 59047
(406) 222-7057
www.ctmarchitects.com

(p. 208) **Donald Rattner**
Studio for Civil Architecture
462 Broadway, 3rd floor
New York, NY 10013
(212) 625-3336
www.thecivilstudio.com

(p. 226) **Peter Zimmerman**
Peter Zimmerman Architects
828 Old Lancaster Road
Berwyn, PA 19312
(610) 647-6970
www.pzarchitects.com

(p. 246) **Ignacio Salas-Humara**
Lopez Salas Architects
1617 East Commerce Street, Suite 7101
San Antonio, TX 78205
(210) 734-4448
www.lopezsalas.com

Russell Versaci
Russell Versaci Architecture, PO Box 186,
7 North Liberty Street,
Middleburg, VA 20118
(540) 687-8777
www.russellversaci.com